HOW TO SEND YOUR
STUDENT TO COLLEGE
WITHOUT LOSING YOUR MIND
OR YOUR MONEY

SHELLEE HOWARD

www.collegereadyplan.com

ISBN-13: 978-1546749622
ISBN-10: 1546749624

Acknowledgements

This book is dedicated to my two amazing children, Ryan and Makena. You both inspire me every day to be the best I can be. Without you, this book would never have been written. Your desire to help others inspired me to write this book, and your support and accountability helped me finish it. You are both living your dream, and I hope to inspire other students to find their passion and never give up on what they want.

To my parents who taught me at an early age that I can do anything if I want it badly enough. The gift of tenacity has helped me throughout my life. Your love and support helped me to be confident enough to be the first in our family to go to college.

To my many long-suffering friends who listened, provided feedback, and were readers of this manuscript. To my new friends I have made along the way and to my coach: each of you have given me invaluable advice and support.

Thank you to the many families who have hired and trusted me with their children's futures. I have learned so much from each and every student I have had the honor of working with. I will always treasure the laughter and the tears, but most of all the grateful hugs and thank you's I have received from my clients.

Harvard graduation 2016

Table of Contents

Introduction

Student debt has just reached an all-time high amounting to $1.4 trillion dollars! Kids are getting out of college with tens of thousands of dollars in debt that they can't pay off while supporting themselves. Many have had to move back in with their parents to make ends meet. It's an enormous problem that families are struggling with.

I wrote this book because I don't want families to struggle. In my book, I am going to show you exactly how your child can go to the college of their dreams without paying full price and in many cases, even go to college debt-free.

You'll also discover my top tips on how to create a successful application, why your student can afford to go to college, and the secrets about free money and scholarships. This book will prevent you from making costly mistakes that the majority of families make.

I'd like to take a minute to introduce myself and tell you how I came to be a College Consultant and expert in this area...

My name is Shellee Howard and I grew up in California. I was the first child to go to college on both sides of my family; I had no guidance but a lot of determination. I graduated from college in four years despite changing my major five times because I attended summer school and winter session. I made so many costly mistakes that I promised myself that my children would not make them too. Instead, they would have a bulletproof plan.

Four days after I graduated from college, I started working in sales for Procter and Gamble and was fortunate to go through all of their first-class training programs. I climbed right through the corporate ceiling in eight years and then had my children. I dedicated myself to being the best mom I could be while still working part time.

Fast forward to my son's 8th grade year, and my story becomes more interesting...

Half way through 8th grade at a public school, my son informs me that he would like to be a brain surgeon. I felt the pressure immediately; I had no idea how to help him! I started with his soon to be high school counselor who told him, *"Why would you want to go to school for that long and incur so much debt?"* I realized at that moment, I was on my own. Feeling defeated, I put on my "mom" face and told him I would take care of it and just stay focused on getting good grades and finding his passion.

Fast forward to his senior year in high school. Not only did my son listen to everything that was advised, he worked his plan. He applied to twelve universities half being Ivy schools. Of those he was accepted into eleven of them and of those he received a free education at half of them. After his list of acceptances was announced, I had people calling me and asking for a plan and advice.

At that point, I went back to college and got my college counseling certification from UCSD. I worked for a college consulting company for several years and then decided to live my dream. I founded my company, College Ready, and have helped hundreds of students get into the college of their dreams debt free!

In fact, this year my daughter started in the Nursing program at the University of Alabama (her dream school) and my son graduated from Harvard debt free in four years. He has since applied to medical school and will be attending UCSD medical school this fall. This is just a snapshot of my journey.

I have helped hundreds of families all over the world get into and graduate from the college of their dreams debt free. Desire is the key, if your student has it... with planning and strategy, they will

2

obtain it! Every student is unique and comes with gifts, talents and opportunities. Together, I help families create a plan that allows the student to stand out and shine among their competition. My proven strategy is successful with all students from Ivy League, to B average students. There is a perfect college waiting for your child and I will help you find it.

What you do not know will cost you, both in time and money.

Take for example, a student (client) of mine, Michael.

Michael came to me as a Freshman and had no idea where he wanted to go to college or what he wanted to major in. He had a strong GPA, but not in the most challenging classes. He had not done any test prep but tested well on his first PSAT. He enjoyed doing community service but was more of a follower than a leader. In just three short years, Michael will graduate this Spring with 9 college offers to choose from. Several of his choices he could attend debt free. Having a plan, Michael was not overwhelmed by the process. He followed the College Ready plan and made adjustments along the way. He now knows, his dream college and major but more importantly he knows what he wants to do after he graduates from college because we took the time to help Michael grow in all areas of his life. There are a lot of stories just like Michael's from students who have graduated from college in four years debt free because they had a plan.

You and your student can be one of these success stories...but only if you plan and if you start now.

You may be thinking that your son or daughter is only a Freshman and that you have "plenty of time". Nothing could be further from the truth. Many of my clients have been with me since the summer before high school. They started with their college plans from day one of high school, which has allowed them to be stress-free and not make any costly mistakes. If your son or daughter is a sophomore, Junior or Senior, it is not too late, but timing is critical. The longer you wait to plan, the more money college will cost your family.

Reading this book will show you how NOT to make the costly mistakes so many families do. It will give you knowledge about college admission as well as finances. I promise you that after you read this book, you will be armed with the knowledge and tools you need so your child can go to college paying as little as possible.

FREE GIFT

As a way of saying thank you to my readers, I have a very special gift for you! My mini eBook, *15 Ways to Get a Reduced or Free College Tuition*.

You can download it now by going to my website:

http://collegereadyplan.com/sign-up/

5

CHAPTER 1

Valuable Lessons: What You Don't Know Is Costing You

Here is your first and most valuable lesson: Did you know that you do not have to pay full price for college?

There are few things more depressing than researching your student's first choice college to find out that the cost of attendance is out of reach. The sticker price can be shocking, and it has brought many parents to tears. Paying for college has just emerged as one of "America's Top Fears."

This chapter will help to put your mind at ease. The only families that pay "full price" for college naively do not know any better.

Let me ask you a question: Would you allow your 17 or 18-year-old to buy a car without being involved in the process? Or even crazier: Would you allow them to purchase a new home without your advice?

One year of college can be the equivalent of buying a new car! Your student's four-year degree can be equivalent to purchasing a new home. If your student picks the wrong college or the wrong major, the cost can be equivalent to that of a new home and a new car.

The cost of attending college gets more expensive every year, even as students struggle with debt and paying for school. Over the past 20 years, tuition and fees at national universities – both private and public – have risen sharply. According to the U.S. Bureau of Labor Statistics, there was a 55.1% increase from 1995 to 2015. During this time period, the average tuition and fees at private national universities jumped 179%. Out-of-state tuition and fees at public universities have risen 226% since 1995, and in-state tuition and fees at public national universities grew the most – increasing a staggering 296%.

Tuition Growth at National Universities
Average tuition and fees at ranked schools, 1995-2015

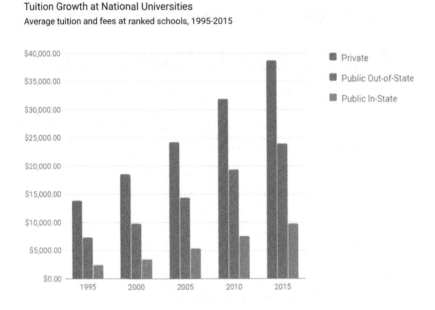

Source: U.S. Bureau of Labor Statistics

When it comes to paying for your child's college education, you may consider some alternatives: You could borrow, borrow, and borrow some more; students are graduating with an average of $35,000 in student loan debt. You could pull the money from your retirement or home equity. Alternatively, you could tell your student that they cannot attend college because you simply cannot afford it.

When it comes to paying for college, the choices can be overwhelming, which is why it's so important to understand all of your options. In reality, about two-thirds of students who attend either a public or private college or university don't pay full price. This is thanks to federal and state grants, as well as institutional awards. The schools that provide the most money and awards will typically be liberal arts and baccalaureate colleges, as well as master's-level universities where there are few Ph.D. programs. In contrast, the schools least likely to provide merit scholarships are research universities.

When it comes to paying for your child's higher education, here is your best option: Planning.

Planning is the key to finding the perfect college, picking the correct major, graduating in four years' debt free, and having a job waiting for your student when he or she graduates.

Yes, all this is possible. And I have many happy parents and students that can prove it!

Let me share two of my students' stories.

COLLEGE READY CASE STUDY #1: PLANNING TO PAY

The first student, I will call Steven, and the second student, I will call Annie. (Names have been changed for privacy reasons).

Steven was raised by a loving, middle class family in California. Neither parent attended college, and the thought of sending a son to college scared them to the point that the subject was never discussed in their home. That said, Steven was on his own to figure out his future. He was a star soccer athlete in high school and on a club soccer team. His dream was to get an athletic scholarship and go to any college that would allow him to play his sport and go to college for free. His parents had managed to put away $32,000 for his college education in a 529 plan, which could only be used for college fees.

The first semester of Steven's high school senior year, he was injured just before his athletic season started. He would not be able to play high school or club sports. He was not too concerned because he already had two verbal commitments from colleges.

However, as the semester progressed, Steven became depressed. He was not able to play the sport he loved, and he had no motivation to go to school. His grades were so bad; he almost did not graduate from high school. The two verbal promises never came to fruition.

Steven's future did not look good. He pulled away from all of his friends who were excited about attending college and started hanging out with a tough crowd. His parents did not know what to do to help Steven, so they went to his high school counselor for advice. They were told it was "too late for Steven to apply to any colleges," and that, "he would have to go to community college and apply next year." In turn, Steven's parents were upset that they let their son down by failing to plan.

Annie, on the other hand, had a different experience. She had two parents who both worked very hard to provide for their family. One parent had attended college, and the other had retired from the military. Annie was self-motivated and driven to succeed. Her dream was to become an Emergency Room Doctor.

Since both of Annie's parents were busy with their careers, they knew they did not have the time to help Annie with her college plans. They hired an Independent College Consultant. Annie worked with her College Coach starting the summer of her 8th grade year. Her College Coach helped her map out every class she would take—from her freshman year to her senior year in high school. They put together a test prep plan with a timeline of each test and when she would take them. They came up with a community service project Annie was passionate about and could lead. They discussed clubs and organizations and how to balance everything she wanted to do. They even considered how they would leverage her sport to complete the college plan.

Annie had a plan starting with her first class in high school. She followed her plan that was created for her strengths and opportunities. She took each test in the proper sequence and timing. Her service project impacted so many lives that it was written about in the local newspaper.

Annie applied to fourteen colleges perfectly selected just for her and for her dream of becoming a doctor. She was accepted into eleven colleges. Ten of them offered her a FULL ride (tuition free) education! Annie was now in charge of her future and got to choose which college she would call her home for the next four years. Her parents used the money they had saved for her undergrad tuition to pay for her medical school.

Annie had no debt after she graduated from college and medical school.

You may be in disbelief, but both of these stories are 100% true. There are hundreds of examples of planning (or a lack thereof) just like these.

Having a plan for your student's academics, testing, community service, leadership, and family finances will allow your family the same opportunity Annie had. Just as no two students are the same, no two families are exactly the same. You do not have to lose your mind and your bank account while going through the college planning process.

This chapter will go on to show you why you do NOT need to pay full price for college. It will give you ways to get a wonderful college degree without paying sticker price or going into debt.

At this point you may be asking yourself: how do I find the best college deals?

SOME GREAT WAYS TO DECREASE THE COST OF COLLEGE:

1. **A Strong GPA (your students weighted grades 10-11th grade) is the best way to get into college and attend for free.** Many colleges all over the country offer a free education to get valedictorians, the top 10 percent, and students who have demonstrated strong leadership skills. Every school is looking for the best students. In the college world, reputation is everything. Schools are looking to graduate the best and brightest students to attract the next generation.

2. **Test scores can get your student a free college education.** Score well on your PSAT, and become a Merit finalist (Scholar, Finalist or Semi –Finalist). Achieving the best scores on the PSAT will open many doors. Colleges – both private and public – will be contacting you and offering you tuition, room and board, etc. This is one of my favorite options to share with my students. I believe it empowers them to think big and to know that if they work hard to succeed on these tests, they can earn a college education for free.

3. **Take dual enrollment or AP classes.** By taking dual enrollment classes while still in high school a student saves on the cost of a college class. In a lot of cases, you can start college at a Sophomore level and save a year of tuition. Taking the AP tests with a score of three or better will give students the opportunity to skip several basic college classes. By choosing either option, you will save both time and money. For more information on dual enrollment, you can find what you need from the National Center for Education Statistics.

4. **Look for colleges with strong merit scholarships.** There are many colleges that offer large merit scholarships to attract great students. These can range from a few thousand dollars up to full tuition, room, and board. Getting a merit scholarship is not easy. Most schools will have you compete for them by writing an essay or going through an interview process. Usually, private colleges offer larger merit scholarships because they can. Most private universities have a strong alumni association that donates millions of dollars to help the college attract strong students. It is also important to consider less selective schools because they tend to offer better merit scholarships in order to appeal to the top students.

If your student has a high GPA or test scores, there is no reason they cannot get a FREE education.

Would you like to go to college for FREE?

1. Focus on YOUR GPA.

2. Focus on YOUR TEST SCORES.

3. Look for colleges that offer Merit Scholarships.

4. Research colleges that reward AP/IB/Dual enrollment.

5. Apply to colleges who meet 100% of your need.

Even state schools can be expensive. It is important to consider the entire package. The cost of attendance, years to graduate, alumni connections, and the success rate of getting a job out of college.

1. **Choose a college your student will graduate from in 4 years.** The vast majority of American college students do not graduate on time. By not graduating in four years, it is costing students and their parents millions of extra dollars. Every additional year it takes your student to graduate from a public four-year college will cost an average $22,826. It is important for your family to know the graduation rate for all the colleges being considered before making the decision to send in the application. Keep in mind: for every additional year it takes your student to graduate, it will also cost them in loss of salary, retirement, company car, and promotion timing. Look for private colleges that have a proven track record of getting their students out in four years. If you plan properly in high school, your student can graduate from college in three years. There are classes that your student can take in high school that will count for college. There are also accelerated college programs with majors that will allow you to graduate in three years.

2. **Look for out-of-state public colleges or international schools with special pricing for out-of-state students.** Many out of state schools offer "special pricing" for out-of-

state students. They will either give you the cost of tuition equal to an in-state student or reduce costs to attract students with a diverse background. Several out-of-state colleges offer merit scholarships for out-of-state students based on their GPA and test scores. If your student is willing to go to college out-of-state, there are many schools that will offer them outstanding scholarships. Think outside the box! You may also want to consider International schools like KTH Royal Institute of Technology where you can get a free technological education.

3. **Look for private schools that meet 100% of need.** Do not ever let your financial need keep your student from attending college. Since every family has a different financial situation, this can be challenging to understand. I will try to simplify this for you.

HOW TO DISCOVER YOUR EXPECTED FAMILY CONTRIBUTION
A FINANCIAL AID TOOL

- First: Go online and pull up a college your student would like to attend.

- Second: Find the financial aid section of the website.

- Third: Search for the EFC (Expected Family Contribution) calculator.

- Fourth: Enter the information that is requested, and press enter.

- Finally: The calculator will provide you with your family's *Expected* amount of money that you will be asked to pay for that college.

If your EFC is $15,000, you will be expected to pay that college $15,000. If the tuition is $30,000, you will have to pay $15,000 (your expected contribution) and you will have to figure out how you will pay for the rest.

At many private colleges, they have a generous alumni group and strong financial backing. Often, they will offer to pay 100% of what you cannot pay over your EFC. So, if your EFC is 0, you can go to many colleges for FREE! There are more of these colleges than you are probably aware of, and they do not advertise their giving. The U.S. News and world report in 2015 stated that 66 colleges claimed to meet 100 percent of demonstrated financial need for full-time, degree-seeking undergraduates. If you can get into these schools and can prove you can't afford it, they will pay for what you can not based on your EFC.

An educated college consultant will know where to find them. With all that said: Planning is the key to lowering your EFC. It is possible and completely legal.

Top 6 Factors to Calculate your EFC

1. Parents income (both even if divorced)

2. Parents assets (both even if divorced)

3. Students income

4. Students assets

5. Number of People in the Household

6. Number of Students in College

---

1. **Look for four-year colleges that your student may commute to, so you will not have to pay for housing and meals.** The cost of living at college is expensive, and it's not usually rolled into the cost to attend. Living on campus can range from $8,000 to $15,000 per year. Look for colleges you can drive to, and plan your schedule to attend classes only a few days a week. Another money saving option is to take online classes. This will not give you the "full college experience," but if money is what is keeping you from going to college, it is another option to consider.

2. **Take advantage of local community colleges for summer school and winter break.** When your student is home for the winter break or summer, consider having him or her sign up to take a class or two at your local community college. This will allow your student to take some basic classes at a reduced price. It could also empower your student to graduate on time or early. This is a great plan to save time and money.

But keep in mind: community colleges are overcrowded. You must register as soon as the courses are released. The US Department of Education reported that a dismal 18% of students who attend just community college right after high school get their 4-year degree. According to the Hechinger Report, fewer than one out of five students at community colleges obtain their desired degree in three years or less. The National Center for Education Statistics shows that only 13% of community college students graduate in two years.

1. Work while attending college, or join the military. There are several colleges that let you work while attending college in exchange for free tuition. Or, you may want to consider committing to one of the nation's military academies or military colleges where you can attend college for free.

Planning and research are critical to this process. In this case, not knowing where to find the best deals on college will cost you! Looking at your planning options earlier in the process will help steer your student away from overpriced colleges so that he or she may focus on strong colleges where they will receive a free or reduced fee.

It is helpful to use charts and lists for college planning like the one included for colleges you are considering here:

Colleges you are considering?

Name of College	EFC	Scholarships	% that graduate in 4 years

BE YOUR OWN ADVOCATE FOR FINANCIAL PLANNING

Our Nation is functioning under a $1 trillion debt crisis! This is out of control, and you do not want your student to be a statistic. For the first time ever, the national student loan default rate exceeds the credit card delinquency rate. Also, note that student loans are one of the few types of debt that cannot be discharged with bankruptcy! If you plan properly, you do NOT need to get a student loan, and you do NOT need to go into debt! It is important that you are careful whom you listen to. Not everyone has all the facts and the correct information. One step you can take is to hire a college consultant who can help you avoid the national crisis that comprises the staggering cost of college.

Don't become a statistic! Before your student applies to any college, I highly suggest you discuss the following topics:

1. **Assess Family finances.**

   College is a huge investment in time and resources. You will want to discuss openly what monies have been saved for college, what you as parents are willing to pay, the possibilities of loans and debt, and which colleges are a good fit financially. If you are not comfortable discussing this with your student, you will need to decide on what you are willing to do to support your student.

   I have met many parents who are worried that their child is only going to college to get out of the house and party. I have the perfect suggestion for these parents! Discuss your concerns with your student, and offer to make them a deal. If they pick a college that does not make sense financially, you can either tell them No, or you can offer to meet them halfway.

   Some of my clients have made a deal that the student may attend the college of their choice and take out a loan to pay for it. If the student graduates with a certain GPA determined by the parent, the parent will pay off the student loan. This is obviously a judgment call by the parent.

2. **Decide whether the student's desired college is a want or a need.**

   Why does the student want to attend a certain college? Is it because their boyfriend or their best friend is going to attend there? Is it because they have a great football team or Greek system? Try to get your student to verbalize why they want to attend a certain college. Write a list of pros and cons! Then ask them if their choice makes sense financially, compared to all of their other options. Is it worth starting their adult life with debt?

3. **Determine if the major they pick will pay for their wants and needs after they graduate.**

Picking the wrong major can be costly. On average, most students change their major 3 times while attending college. If not done properly or with a plan, these changes can cost you both time and money.

4. Before your student picks a major, ask them to write down 10 things they are passionate about.

10 Passions

1.

2.

3.

4.

5.

6.

7.

8.

9.

10.

Set that list of passions aside for the time being. But do follow up with asking your student what he or she would like to major in and why. If your student is unsure and has little or no direction, consider that a red flag! I recommend that you work with your student to figure out their passion or seek the advice of a professional. This will cost them time and money. Especially if your child selects a college based on what they "think they want to major in." Not every college has every major. Picking a college based on a *maybe I want to do something* attitude is asking for trouble.

Ask your student to pick three majors and make sure each college they apply to offers at least two of their options. Changing majors while in school may mean taking unnecessary classes, which means wasted money.

Majors to consider:

- Accounting
- Agricultural Studies
- Anthropology
- Archaeology
- Architecture/Environmental Design
- Arts
- Astronomy
- Aviation
- Biological Sciences
- Business Administration/Finance/Marketing
- Chemistry
- Communications
- Computer Science
- Criminology
- Cultural Studies
- Design/Fashion/Interior
- Economics

- Education
- Engineering
- English/Writing/Journalism
- Environmental Studies
- Geology/Earth Science
- Government
- Health Sciences
- History
- Hospitality
- International Studies
- Philosophy
- Physical Education
- Physical Sciences
- Physics
- Political Science
- Pre-Professional Studies (Dental, Engineering, Law, Medicine and Vet)
- Protection Services
- Psychology
- Public Policy
- Religious Studies/Theology
- Social Services
- Sociology
- Speech Communication
- Theatre/Drama
- Tourism
- Transportation

Again, a plan is very important. Finally, based on your specific major, there are plenty of follow up questions to consider:

- What does your student want to do after graduation?

- What are your student's career goals and aspirations?

Starting with the end in mind will save your student a ton of time and money. If your student picks a career that you know will never be able to pay back their college debt—Consider this another Red Flag!

It is time to start from the beginning and discuss the cost of living on their own and taking care of their family. Try not to shoot down their dreams while still being realistic about their future.

1. **Note the graduation rate of the colleges your student is considering.**

   Less than 1/3 of all public and non-profit four-year colleges have a 4-year graduation rate of 50% or better. What does this mean to your student? Each additional year will cost more money. Not only will the additional year be an added expense, it will also take money away from your student. No salary for an additional year, no retirement for an additional year, no health insurance for an additional year. A low graduation rate usually means that the college is over-crowded, and students cannot get the classes they need to fulfill their requirements.

2. **Learn about the acceptance rates at the colleges your student would like to apply to.**

   Acceptance rates show supply and demand for a specific school. A school with a low acceptance rate means that it is in high demand and will most likely not be offering many merit scholarships.

3. **Consider the size of the college.**

   Approximately three-quarters of all colleges have less than 5,000 undergraduates. Most students prefer colleges larger than 5,000 students. There are many more smaller schools than there are large schools. Because the larger schools are better known, they do not have to offer money to compete. You are more likely to get a better financial package at a small school.

4. Know that other add-ons to college add up.

Beyond tuition as well as room and board, please consider these expenses when completing your budget: Health insurance, gym fees, parking and car registration, activity fees, dorm damage deposit, computer insurance, dorm room stuff, technology fees, lab fees, Greek life, spending money, travel money, and quite possibly the most expensive add-on...the cost of books.

On the following page there is a tool to help you plan for college.

College Fact Finding Chart

Complete for each college you are considering:

College Name
Location
Public or Private
Religious Affiliation
Number of Undergrads
Freshman Retention Rate
Academic Programs
Challenging / Moderate / Easy
Class Size
Majors of Interest
Student Body
Appearance / Style
Dorms
Library
High Speed Internet Student Center
Athletic Program and Workout Complex
Social Life or Fraternities / Sororities
Active Campus Life
Off-Campus Activities
Job Placement
Roommate Finder
Proximity to airport
Special Programs
Student/Faculty Ratio
Tutoring
Safety
Diversity
Housing
Food
Weather
Cost and Financial Aid Accreditation
Pre-requisites for freshman enrollment
Do Professors or TA's teach the classes

When you buy a house, you hire experts like a realtor, banker, broker, escrow agent, etc. When you pay your taxes, you hire a professional accountant. Trying to navigate this college process alone can make you crazy. The reality is that even with all the information you can find online, you do not know what is reliable. You do not have an expert offering you suggestions on what you can do to NOT go into debt. This process can be scary and over-whelming for your family. But knowledge equals stress relief and savings.

There is so much to know about the college application process and what you do not know will cost you and your student both time and money.

If you would like to save yourself a lot of time and frustration, contact College Ready for a free 30-minute consultation to see if your student can get a FREE or reduced college education.

To Schedule Your Free Consultation, go to:
http://collegereadyplan.com/free-call/

CHAPTER 2

Preparing For College: Why It Really Matters

It's time to get honest with yourself and your student's path to college. Reflect truthfully on these important questions for your college journey:

- Does your student know what colleges he or she is looking for?

- Does your student know how long it takes for each application to be read?

- Does your student know when he or she should start the application process?

- Does your student know what GPA he or she needs to get into the college of his or her dreams?

- Does your student know what is better – Honors, AP, IB, or Dual Enrollment?

- Does your student know which standardized test is the best for him or her – SAT or ACT?

- Does your student know when to take each test and how to test prep?

- Does your student know what a fee waiver is?

- Does your student know how many community service hours he or she needs?

- Does your student know that not all service hours are created equal?

- Does your student know that Leadership is important to his or her college acceptance?

- Does your student know how many colleges to apply to and how to decide which schools are a good match?

- Does your student know that an entrance essay has the potential to be a deal breaker?

- Does your student know if a campus tour or a college interview is important for his or her particular schools?

The reality is: if your student cannot answer YES to all these questions, then your student is NOT College Ready. That said, this chapter is going to be the most important chapter of this book.

Chapter 1 discussed the importance of planning. But, are you ready to learn the secret weapon that parents use to send their student to college without losing their mind or your money? It's **KNOWLEDGE**.

Let's start getting to know what you need to know to be College Ready.

So, your student has decided they would like to apply to college. Congratulations! You must be so excited and proud of their decision.

For some parents, this process may be scary, overwhelming, and possibly dreadful. As a parent and counselor, I aim to guide you and your student on a path to a successful college application season.

If you attended college more than 10 years ago, you will be surprised at how much the process and cost has changed. Since I was the first child in my family to go to college (and I applied to college in 1985), I understand any apprehensive feelings about the application process.

However, some modern-day experience with college applications has armed me to help you. My first-born applied to college in 2012 and to medical school in 2016. My youngest child applied to college in 2016 and is currently looking to transfer schools for her major and chosen career goal. I consult with hundreds of students all over the world, and there is one thing they all have in common: the fear of applying to and paying for college.

One of the first things I learned about college applications: this process is nothing like it used to be. Gone are the good ol' days that you could pay your way into a college. Gone are the days that you took one standardized test – just one time – and submitted one score. Gone are the days that you could attend community college while figuring out your major, get your AA in two years, and transfer into a university to finish your degree in a total of four years. Gone are the days when you could pre-register for classes and get the classes you wanted. Gone are the days that you could work and pay for your own college education. Long gone are the days when you could get into a college based on your GPA alone. Gone, too, are the days when you could get a full ride scholarship for your sport.

So much has changed in just 10 years.

Remember, that applying to college is competitive. It's a process that should be taken seriously. The time your student puts into the college application process will be worth the effort. Do not assume anything as you proceed to educate yourself on what your student's options are. What you *do not know* in this process will cost you and your student.

WHEN SHOULD YOUR STUDENT START PREPARING FOR COLLEGE?

This is one of the top five questions I get everytime I speak to a large audience. The answer is quite simple: You should start when your child is ready and shows interest.

In my line of work, I often encounter many people who are interested in my son's journey to Harvard. As soon as someone finds out that my son got into Harvard and graduated in four-years debt free, they want the magic secret! I hate to be the bearer of bad news, but there is no secret. Good behaviors, habits, hard work, and passion is what will lead your student to a dream school.

After being a College Consultant for more than seven years, I have seen a pattern emerge in the students who are successful in getting into the college of their dreams. Here are several things I have seen time and time again:

- **Teach your student to love reading and knowledge from an early age.** I am not suggesting that you become obsessive with a toddler's education. However, an early introduction to books they enjoy can have a great impact for the future. You can also be an example as a reader yourself. Read to them, and when they are old enough, have them read to you. This may sound simple, but establishing a love for learning will help them enjoy school all the way through college.

- **Talk to your student about your college experience and your alma mater.** Tell them stories about how much you enjoyed college. This sets the tone for future conversation and questions about college.

- **When you are on a family vacation, take a half-day and tour a nearby college**. Let your student see what college life is like and why it is important for them to attend college. College is not for everyone, but at the early stages of childhood, sharing knowledge is the key to having options.

When it comes to a personal enjoyment of education: this will happen at different times for each student. If you have a student who enjoys learning, then I suggest you put them into a college prep school or the GATE program at a public school. The goal is to keep the student challenged and enjoying learning. The key here is not to push the child or force them, but to support and guide them. Balance is the key to a lifetime of learning.

Pursuing passions is a huge part of preparing to go to college. Most kids are already showing interest in particular hobbies at a young age, and it is important to expose children to a variety of activities. Time-wise, most students will know their gifts and talents by middle school. Continue to encourage your student to try new things. The classes they take in middle school will set them up for their high school academic experience.

Seek some academic support as soon as you realize your student may need help in one subject or across the curriculum. It is unrealistic to think that if your student struggles in math, that they will be allowed to take the more challenging math classes in high school. Your student will be tested along the way, and these tests will be used to assess where your student will be placed in high school. If your student is struggling in one subject, it is recommended to get a tutor as soon as you are able. Math, for example, is a building block. If a student struggles in pre-algebra, he or she will find algebra 1 and algebra 2 very difficult. Always make sure your student masters the fundamentals before moving on too quickly.

In English, the same can be true. If a student struggles with sentence structure, he or she will not want to write essays in high school and college. This may seem fundamental, but this is where many parents make mistakes with shaping their students' schedules. Pushing a student to move on to the next level too quickly will stress out the student and can cause future problems.

Eighth grade is truly when a student's college application starts. No, your student will not list all eighth-grade classes or grades. However, be aware that your student will get the opportunity to take high school level classes in middle school. These courses are like a gateway; they will allow students to start high school at an advantage. Taking classes like advanced math, English and a foreign language are ways to get ahead. If your student takes pre-algebra in 8th grade, they will get to start high school in algebra etc. Every class counts!

COLLEGE READY CASE STUDY: Preparing to Succeed

Let me share a true story about two students who attended two different middle schools but the same public high school. The first student, Shannon, attended a private elementary and middle school; she transferred to a public high school in 9th grade. The second student, Tyler, attended a public middle school and the same public high school as Shannon.

Shannon had the opportunity to take pre-algebra and Spanish 1 in middle school, so she started high school in algebra 1 and Spanish 2. Tyler also took pre-algebra, but he was not able to take a foreign language because he chose to be in leadership at his middle school.

Tyler started high school in algebra 1 and Spanish 1. No AP or IB classes were offered at their school their freshman year. Both students continued to take the most challenging schedule of classes that were offered at their school. Both Shannon and Tyler received A's in every high school class they took.

During the final week of their senior year, the class ranking was announced, and this is when reality set in. Shannon was announced as the valedictorian, and Tyler was the salutatorian. The difference between 1st in their class and 2nd in their class was starting with Spanish 1 vs. Spanish 2.

The happy ending here is that both students went on to the colleges of their dreams. But this real-life example is meant to show how important class selection and planning is.

Getting into college today is challenging and costly. Not preparing properly will cost your student college acceptances as well as money.

So, where does your student begin? As stated before, 8th graders need to consider their high school schedule.

The college application actually starts with the listing of the first high school classes. Every schedule – from the fall of their freshman year – to the spring of their senior year are all very important. Every student must complete all classes necessary to graduate from high school. There is a list of classes that every student must take, and then there are classes that colleges require. Knowing this information before planning a high school schedule is critical to the final results. Many high schools hold orientations for incoming freshmen in the spring.

Please do not leave class schedule planning to your 14-year-old student! Many students will either pick the easy classes, classes with their best friends, and classes that sound fun. *Your involvement is critical at this point.* The high school may tell your student they are not smart enough for a class or that the class is already full. Your student may be told that they ought to take a certain class next academic year. It is critical that you be an advocate for your student.

Children have been taught to respect their elders, so when an adult tells them no, they often accept the no. More than 50% of the students I mentor have dealt with this situation in some fashion. Parents may need to be an advocate for their student if necessary.

As a mother of two, I had to sit down with my own children's high school administration every semester. I understand that high schools are dealing with thousands of students and that they have guidelines and rules. What I will never understand is why the interest of the student does not come first. I was told by school administration: "that cannot happen," at least three times during my son's four years in high school. Guess what? After I spoke with the Principal and explained my son's situation, arrangements were made to accommodate his needs.

AN ANECDOTE ON BEING YOUR OWN ADVOCATE:

During my son's junior year in high school, he was told that there was no way to take the math he needed and the English he needed because there were not enough teachers teaching both AP classes. I was told that the classes were full due to the limited AP classes that were offered. My son tried to fix this situation on his own, but he was told no. Instead of letting it go, we went in as a team and spoke to his high school counselor. We were told that there were not any options to take the classes he needed.

My son was frustrated and started talking to other students in his situation. It turned out that there were four students who were affected by the lack of class availability. I called the mother of one of those students, and we made an appointment together with the high school principal. We told her of our students' situation, and instead of telling us no, she listened to our suggestion. We suggested that she allow our students to attend AP 12th grade English their junior year and AP 11th grade English their senior year. Both of these classes had nothing to do with each other in regard to learning the subject, and although it had never been done, the Principal approved the change. Both students were able to get into all the classes they needed to be competitive for the colleges they wanted to apply to.

That said, while I caution parents who hover a little too close to their student, it is helpful to know when and how to step in for your child's education. We did not go into this meeting demanding that the changes be made, we simply stated our case and gave our suggestion. I would have preferred that my son handle this himself, but in reality, it was more than he was prepared to handle.

The bottom line is that every student is different. Each student has unique needs. If there is a plan in place, your student will receive the education they need to be successful. I believe that a successful education is the common desire for you, for your student, and for the higher education institutes too. Working the plan together will get your student the education they want and need. This teamwork will also set them up for the college application success.

Do you have a plan in place? Can you answer all the questions in this chapter? If not, do not worry! By reading this book you receive a free 30-minute consultation where you can get your questions answered! To Schedule Your Free Consultation, go to: http://collegereadyplan.com/free-call/.

CHAPTER 3

Standing Out: The Top 3 Things Colleges Are Looking For These Days

As I mentioned in Chapter 2, gone are the good ol' days of submitting one college application; today is a new era for education. The world is changing at a rapid pace, and so are the criteria for colleges.

Here are the top 3 things colleges are looking for right now:

1. **What GPA will my student need to get into college?**

   Your student's GPA is absolutely the KING in the college application process! Most colleges will look at your student's weighted GPA. Let me help explain the difference so you will have a better understanding of what colleges look at when reviewing your student's application.

   The un-weighted GPA: Traditionally, your student's Grade Point Average (GPA) is calculated on an un-weighted scale. It is measured on a scale of 0 to 4.0. It does NOT take into account the difficulty of a student's coursework. When your student receives an A, it is considered a 4.0, whether it was earned in an Honors/AP class or a lower level class.

The weighted GPA: This is often used by high schools to better represent students' academic accomplishments. The weighted GPA takes into account *course difficulty* rather than providing the same letter grade to each student. Usually, weighted GPA is measured on a scale of 0 to 5.0, although some scales go up higher. An A in an Honors or AP class may translate into a 5.0 weighted GPA, while an A in a low-level class will give you a 4.0 weighted GPA. Many schools also have mid-level classes where the highest weighted GPA you can earn is a 4.5.

For the most part, whether your high school uses un-weighted or weighted GPA shouldn't affect you in the college application process. Colleges will look at your GPA, but they will also consider the bigger picture. The school's greatest concern is that your student has managed to challenge him or herself intellectually through coursework.

2. Is rigor important?

In other words: Should your student take Honors, AP, IB, or Dual enrollment classes and get B's, or should they take a regular schedule and get all A's?

I wish the answer was that simple. It all depends on if your student would like to attend the local state college or an Ivy League university. What does he or she want to major in during college? What are the student's strengths and opportunity subjects? This is where planning is critical. Knowing what kind of college your student would like to attend before planning their classes will save time, money, and a lot of frustration.

Many times students come to me in their junior year and tell me that they would like to attend an Ivy League school, but they have not taken any challenging classes. The reality is: most likely, an Ivy League school will not be a good fit. The more difficult a college is to get into, the more competition there is going to be to get into that college. To be competitive, a student must take the most rigorous classes they can take, and he or she must earn the best grades possible.

It would not be a good fit to take a student who has never taken an AP, IB, or college level class before and send them to a top 10 college. Academic life would be difficult, and the student would likely feel that he or she did not fit in. The same would be true if you sent a student who took all AP or IB classes in high school and attended a community college. The fit must be right for a student to thrive in college and to graduate in four years. Planning is the key to how much rigor, how many challenging classes a student should take, and when the student should take them.

A Quick Note on Rigorous Courses: You may be wondering what does AP, IB, or Dual Enrollment mean, and are they important?

AP Stands for Advanced Placement: The definition of an AP class is, "A program in the United States and Canada created by the College Board which offers college-level curricula and examinations to high school students. American colleges and universities may grant placement and course credit to students who obtain high scores on the examinations."

At the end of the AP class, there is an AP examination your student can take. If they get a 3 or better on this test, many things can happen. First, the teacher may give the student an A in the class for fully understanding the subject. Second, the student may not have to take this class in college. Depending on the college they attend, the AP exam may take the place of the college class. This option will save time and money by not having to take an extra college class. Third, if the student is an AP Scholar, which means, "A high school student who has demonstrated exemplary college-level achievement on AP Exams. The student must score a 3 or higher on three or more AP Exams. The AP Scholar with Honor: Is granted to students who receive an average score of at least 3.25 on all AP Exams taken, and scores of 3 or higher on four or more of these exams". What does this mean to your student? Merit scholarships often come from this prestigious award.

See the AP award levels below:

AP Award levels

AP Award	Criteria
AP Scholar:	Awarded to students who receive scores of 3 or higher on 3 or more AP Exams
AP Scholar with Honor:	Awarded to students who receive an average score of at least 3.25 on all AP Exams taken, and scores of 3 or higher on 4 or more of these exams
AP Scholar with Distinction:	Awarded to students who receive an average score of at least 3.5 on ALL AP Exams taken, and scores of 3 or higher on 5 or more of these exams
State AP Scholar:	Awarded to 1 male and 1 female in each U.S. state and the District of Columbia with scores of 3 or higher on the greatest number of AP Exams, and then the highest average score on all AP exams taken (at least 3.5)
National AP Scholar:	Awarded to students in the US who receive an average score of at least 4 on all AP Exams taken, and scores of 4 or higher on 8 or more of these exams
AP Seminar and Research Certificate:	Awarded to students who earn scores of 3 or higher in both AP Seminar and AP Research.
AP Capstone Diploma:	Awarded to students who earn scores of 3 or higher in AP Seminar and AP Research and on 4 additional AP Exams of their choosing.
International AP Scholar:	Awarded to 1 male and 1 female attending a school outside the US and Canada that is not a DoDEA school with the highest average score on the greatest number of AP Exams. Min. requirement is a 3 or higher on 3 exams

IB stands for International Baccalaureate. The definition of the IB programs is as follows: "The program encourages both personal and academic achievement. It aims to challenge students to excel in their studies and in their personal development. This program offers four highly respected programs of education that develop the intellectual, personal, emotional, and social skills needed to live, learn and work in a fast-changing world. The Diploma Program (DP), curriculum is made up of six subject groups and the DP core, comprising theory of knowledge (TOK), creativity, activity, service (CAS) and the extended essay. Through the DP core, students reflect on the nature of knowledge, complete independent research and undertake a project that often involves community service." Not all schools offer the IB program so if your student is interested, they may need to transfer to another school who has been IB authorized.

Dual enrollment: This course work is less common than the AP and IB programs because not all high schools offer this type of program. The definition of the Dual enrollment (DE) programs states that they, "Allow students to be enrolled in two separate, academically related institutions. Generally, it refers to high school students taking college or university courses." Dual enrollment can be advantageous to students because it allows them to get a head start on their college careers. In some cases, the student may even be able to attain an Associate of Arts or equivalent degree shortly before or after their high school graduation. Furthermore, participation in dual enrollment may ease the transition from high school to college by giving students a sense of what college academics are like. In addition, dual enrollment may be a cost-efficient way for students to accumulate college credits, because courses are often paid for by and taken through the local high school.

Who should take these types of classes, and why are they important?

First, NOT all students should take AP, IB or Dual enrollment. Not because a student is not smart, but because these classes move at a rapid pace and teach at a college-level of thinking. This may overwhelm some students with varied learning styles, which could cause their grades in other classes to suffer.

Knowing the type of learner your student is emerges as most important and a critical part of the college planning process. Seek advice from your student's previous teachers. Examine past grades in the subject, and analyze test scores to understand what is best for your student.

Seeking the help of a guidance counselor or college consultant may help guide you to the best path of coursework for your student.

Assess your student with this survey below. See if you learn something new that will help as you plan together.

Student Self Survey

Who are you and what do you want?
Strongly Agree = 4 Agree = 3 Neutral=2 Disagree =1
(write the number next to the question / higher the number = you)

I enjoy listening to and discussing other student's opinions.
I enjoy learning things on my own.
I am excited to go to college.
I enjoy discussing current events.
College will provide me with opportunities.
I honestly enjoy school.
I learn by listening.
I learn by seeing.
I learn by hearing.
I learn by writing.
I am a good listener.
I enjoy public speaking in front of a group.
I am happy spending time alone.
I do no like doing things alone.
I love learning.
I am organized.
I have good time management skills.
I believe the most important reason to go to college is to get a job.
I have at least one school subject that I am passionate about.
I normally love the classes I am taking.
I enjoy learning a foreign language.
School is fun.
I will be sad when I graduate from High School.
I have no problem asking my teacher for help.
There are at least two things I can do better than others.
I look forward to moving away from home.
I enjoy reading I feel I know myself pretty well.
I often participate in class discussions.
I enjoy community service.
I am a better athlete than a student.
I have test anxiety.
I prefer multiple -choice tests.
I prefer essay tests.
I see many benefits to going to college.

3. Are Standardized Test Scores Important?

Parents and students find that standardized testing can be stressful and overwhelming. There are two main tests that colleges consider: The ACT and the SAT. You may wonder if one is better than the other. Frankly, the two tests are equal in the eyes of college admission. In the past, the east coast schools favored the ACT, and the west coast favored the SAT; now most colleges will accept scores from both.

You may be wondering about the PSAT or PLAN. Both of those tests are "pre-tests" to the SAT and ACT. Should your student take both? Yes. If your school offers both, you should have your student take both pre-tests. The pre-tests are great indicators of how your student will score on the SAT and ACT.

Now, here is where I share a big secret with you:

Have your student take the PSAT their freshman year, sophomore year and their junior year.

Why? Most high schools will not inform your student that they can take the pre-tests their freshman and sophomore year. This lack of knowledge will put your student at a disadvantage. My students who have a testing plan know when to take each test and why they are taking the tests in the order recommended.

Standardized testing is not like any other test your student has taken. The first time they take the PSAT, it is intimidating. It can be likened to taking off the training wheels on a bike. They may wobble a little bit, and then they will eventually find good balance.

The pressure students feel the first time they take a standardized test can be overwhelming and humbling. Since the freshman and sophomore PSAT tests do not count for anything, it is the perfect time to practice their testing skills. It is very important for your student to take the PSAT their junior year. I like to call this test the "money round." Some scholarship dollars can be at stake when your student takes the junior year PSAT.

The following information was taken directly from PSAT/NMSQT Student Guide: National Merit® Scholarship Program:

> Students must take the PSAT/NMSQT in the specified year of their high school program. Because a student can participate (and be considered for a scholarship) in only one specific competition year, the year in which the student takes the PSAT/NMSQT to enter the competition is very important.
>
> Different types of scholarships will be offered, but no student can receive more than one monetary award from NMSC. National Merit® $2500 Scholarships. These awards are unique because every Finalist is considered for one and winners are named in every state. The winners are selected by a committee of college admission officers and high school counselors.
>
> Two simple steps could mean money for college:
>
> 1. Take the PSAT/NMSQT or PSAT 10.
>
> 2. Say "yes" to Student Search Service® when you fill out your answer sheet on test day.

National Merit Scholarship Program: When you take the PSAT/NMSQT, you're automatically screened for the National Merit® Scholarship Program, an academic competition for recognition and scholarships. The PSAT 10 and PSAT 8/9 are not considered for entry.

The PLAN: This is also a good practice test, but is not offered at many schools and there is no "money round". The PLAN is a good indicator of how your student may do on the ACT. The best time for your student to take this test is during sophomore year.

How does your student decide which test to take? I always recommend to take the SAT and ACT at least once. Compare the student's scores and you will have a definitive answer. After the tests, a student will receive a breakdown of their scores by category. Please review the assessment with your student. Some questions to review after testing might include:

- Were there any surprises?

- Do the scores represent the student's strengths?

- When a college looks at your student's scores, what will they assume?

- Now comes the really important question – Did your student get the score they need to get into the college of their dreams?

That is the million-dollar question, and since every student has a different dream school, it cannot be answered in a book. It is critical to do the research and find out what past testing scores were needed to get into a particular school.

An additional question to consider after testing: If the student's score does not meet the minimum score needed for a particular school, what can your student do?

Again, planning is everything, and a test prep and testing timeline should be put together to accomplish what is needed by your student. Maybe the student gets test anxiety (which has been proven to be a real thing), or maybe the student was sick when they took the last test. It is now time to make a decision: does your student want to or need to take the test again, or are they willing to choose a less competitive college?

If your student chooses to take the test again, you will need to decide as a family how can they achieve a better score. If the student did not do any test prep before taking the standardized tests, they have many options to increase their score.

- First, they can go to ACT or College board websites and take the practice tests for free online.

- Second, they can buy a test prep book and study from the book.

- Third, they can pay to take a test prep class online.

- Fourth, they can take a test prep class for a nominal fee at their school or library.

- Fifth, you can pay a private test prep tutor to come into your home and work on exactly what your student needs.

- Lastly (the option I strongly recommend): Take a professional test prep class taught by a real test prep teacher.

Let me caution you here. Not all test prep companies are created equal. Educating yourself about your options will save you time, money, and a lot of frustration.

College consultants have statistics on the most successful test prep companies, and they will refer companies that have been successful for past clients. Standardized test prep for the ACT and SAT is more than just discussing the subject on the test. Your student will learn how to take tests. Students will learn how to eliminate answers quickly, find key words in a passage, and so much more. It has been my experience that test prep can make the difference of getting into a State School Vs. a high-ranking university. With good preparation, many of my students have increased their SAT scores by over 300 points.

One last thought on test prep: The skills learned will be used for the rest of their academic career. Every one of my college students have come back to tell me that what they learned in their test prep class has helped them to be a better test taker in college.

SAT vs. ACT? I have heard parents say that a student who is good in math should take the ACT, and a student who is good in English should take the SAT. It has been my experience that these statements just are not true.

Taking the SAT and ACT is the best way to show colleges your student has the skills and knowledge they want most. Most colleges accept both test scores. You should also know that there are "test optional colleges" that do not require applicants to take either test. You may also find that if you only take the ACT, your student may still need to take the SAT subject tests.

Very few students get the same score on both the ACT and SAT. I have a conversion tool to assess your student's strengths on these tests. The SAT and the ACT assess different information and problem solving skills; that is why I recommend your student take both tests at least once. I have outlined the key differences below:

Testing	
Test Format	
SAT:	
Testing Time:	3 hour test (+50 minute essay)
Structure:	3 tests and essay
# of questions:	154
Time per question:	1 minute, 10 seconds
Score range:	composite 400-1600 / essay 2-8
Test timing:	Reading 65 min. / Writing & Lang. 35 min. Math 80 min. / Essay
Test problems:	Reading 52 / Writing & Lang. 44 Math 58
ACT:	
Testing Time:	2 hours 55 minutes (+40 minute essay)
Structure:	4 tests and essay
# of questions:	215
Time per question:	49 seconds
Score range:	composite 1-36 / essay 2-12
Test timing:	Reading 35 min. / English 45 min. Math 60 min. / Science 35 min. / Essay
Test problems:	Reading 40/ English 75 min. Math 60 / Science 40

- **Similarities and differences:**
  - **The SAT:** Originally designed as an aptitude test, it measures students' reasoning and verbal abilities, not material learned in school. The new SAT exam launched in 2016 is much more of an achievement exam than earlier versions of the SAT.

  - **The ACT:** It is an achievement test meant to assess what you have learned in school. This test was designed so that if you study, you should do much better than a student who did not prep.

  - **Test Length:** The SAT takes a little bit longer, but it allows students more time per question than the ACT.

  - **Structural Differences:** The SAT questions get more difficult as they progress. The ACT has a more consistent level of difficulty.

  - **ACT Science:** One of the biggest differences between the ACT and SAT is the ACT has a science section. This section includes questions in areas such as biology, chemistry, earth sciences, and physics. You do not need to be great at science to do well on the ACT. The science section of the test is actually assessing your students' ability to read and understand graphs, scientific hypotheses, and research summaries. Students who do well with critical reading often do well on the Science Reasoning Test.

  - **Writing Skills Differences:** Grammar is important for both the SAT and ACT. Your student must know the rules for subject/verb agreement, proper pronoun usage, identifying run-ons, and so on. However, the emphasis in each exam is a little different. The ACT places more emphasis on punctuation, and it also includes questions on rhetoric strategies.

  - **SAT Vocabulary:** The SAT critical reading sections place more emphasis on vocabulary than the ACT English sections.

- o **ACT Math:** The ACT asks a few questions on trigonometry. The SAT does not. The ACT math section is all multiple-choice. The SAT math section has some questions that require written answers.

- o **The SAT Guessing Penalty:** On the old SAT if you guessed at a question and got it wrong, you were penalized. This changed with the new test released in March 2016. There is now no penalty for guessing on the SAT or ACT.

- o **Essays:** The essay is optional on both the SAT and ACT. But please be aware that many colleges require the essay score. I always recommend that my students sign up and complete the essay on both tests.

- o **Scoring Differences:** The ACT is out of 36 points, whereas each section of the SAT is out of 800 points. Both test scores are weighted so that it's equally hard to get a perfect score on either exam. Average scores are frequently around 500 for the SAT and 21 for the ACT. The main difference between the ACT and the SAT is that the ACT provides a composite score. It shows how your student's combined scores measure up against other test takers. The SAT provides just individual scores for each section. For the ACT, colleges often place more weight on the composite score than individual scores.

Back to the money questions!

Are you eligible for a test fee waiver? (It could save you a ton of money):

SAT fee waivers are available to low-income 11th and 12th grade students in the U.S. SAT Subject Test fee waivers are available for students in grades 9 through 12.

You're eligible for fee waivers if you say "YES" to any of these items:

- o You're enrolled in or eligible to participate in the National School Lunch Program (NSLP).

o Your annual family income falls within the Income Eligibility Guidelines set by the USDA Food and Nutrition Service.

o You're enrolled in a federal, state, or local program that aids students from low-income families (e.g., Federal TRIO programs such as Upward Bound).

o Your family receives public assistance.

o You live in federally subsidized public housing or a foster home, or you are homeless.

o You are a ward of the state or an orphan.

What Fee Waivers Cover

o The registration fee for up to two SATs, with or without the SAT Essay

o The registration fee for up to two SAT Subject Test administrations (take up to three individual SAT Subject Tests on a single test day)

o Four limited-time score reports plus four to use at any time (see details below)

o Four college application fee waivers

o Question-and-Answer Service (QAS) or Student Answer Service (SAS) if ordered at the time of registration (QAS and SAS aren't available for SAT Subject Tests)

o A fee reduction for multiple-choice score verification or essay score verification

o Coverage of the SAT Essay if you are an SAT School Day tester whose school or district covers only the SAT but supports essay testing

o Coverage of the non-U.S. regional fee for fee-waiver-eligible U.S. students who are testing abroad

o Up to eight CSS/Financial Aid PROFILE® fee waivers to use to apply online for nonfederal financial aid from colleges, universities, professional schools, and scholarship programs, for free.

What Fee Waivers Don't Cover: Even if you have a fee waiver, it doesn't cover some of the costs for changing your registration. For example, if you want to change your test center or the date you're taking the SAT, you'll have to pay for that. You also have to pay for rush scores, or to receive your scores by phone.

Apply to Colleges — For Free: Every student who uses an SAT fee waiver gets four college application fee waivers too.

Does Your Student Need To Take The Subject II Tests? There are 20 SAT Subject Tests in five general subject areas: English, history, languages, mathematics and science. Each Subject Test is an hour long. They are all multiple-choice and scored on a 200–800 scale. Subject Tests test your students on their knowledge of subjects at a high school level. The best way to prepare is to take the relevant courses and to work hard in them.

Why your student should take the subject tests:

Colleges May Require Subject Tests: Some colleges require or recommend that you take SAT Subject Tests, especially if you're applying to take specific courses or programs.

Stand Out in College Admissions: Even colleges that don't require Subject Tests may accept them and use them in admission to get a more complete picture of applicants. By sending Subject Test scores to colleges, your student can showcase their strengths.

By taking the tests in your student's strongest subjects, they can show colleges his or her interest in specific majors or programs. Student scores will tell schools if your student is ready to do college level work. Some colleges use the Subject Tests to place students into the appropriate courses. Depending on your student's test scores, they may be able to fulfill basic requirements or get credit for intro-level courses. This will save your student both time and money.

Note for International Students: If your student's English language skills are not strong, they can use Subject Tests to show their academic strength in math, science, or other languages. Also, many international colleges use Subject Tests to make decisions about admission or placement. So, taking the tests gives your student more opportunities. And taking Subject Tests can help your student see how well they have learned the subject matter compared to other students around the world.

Bilingual or multilingual students: If your student speaks a language other than English, SAT Subject Tests are a great opportunity for them to show their skills. Your student may be able to fulfill foreign language competency requirements for some colleges. Be sure to check policies on SAT Subject Tests in foreign languages for the colleges your student is interested in.

Home-schooled students: Some colleges require or recommend SAT Subject Tests for home-schooled applicants to get a better idea of their college readiness. And taking SAT Subject Tests can help your student see how well they have learned the subject matter compared to other students around the country and the world.

In general, your student should take SAT Subject Tests right after they've completed the recommended classes, because the material will still be fresh in their mind. In some cases, this may mean the spring of their freshman or sophomore year. For the language tests, however, it's best to take these tests after they've studied the language for at least two years. Keep in mind, not all Subject Tests are offered on every test date.

Are you unsure of when your student should schedule their SAT Subject Tests? Talk to a college consultant who can advise you the best time to take each test.

The Bottom Line: GPA is the most important factor in the college application process. If your student is hoping to get into a competitive college or university, every class they take will matter. Every class they choose to take must be done in the proper order and receive the best grade possible. Taking a class that is too difficult for your student can backfire with a low grade.

Please have a plan for all four years. Know what classes are needed to graduate as well as what classes colleges are looking for. If one of these assessments does not match the rest in caliber of scores, a new plan must be put into place.

Lastly, standardized testing should match the GPA and rigor. If all three components do not match up on the application, colleges will question what is missing. Planning is the key to success! Every class matters, every grade matters, and every test score matters. If you are not sure if your student's GPA and test scores match, please contact College Ready (www.collegereadyplan.com). We will be happy to do the analysis for you.

CHAPTER 4

Applying: The Ingredients Of A Successful Application

Now that you understand the importance of your student's GPA, rigor, and standardized tests, let me share some other important topics colleges will be considering while reviewing your student's application.

Class Rank: How does your student compare to his or her classmates? The College Board defines class rank as *"a mathematical summary of a student's*

academic record compared to those of other students in the class." Your student's ranking will show how they compare to other students in his or her high school with the same opportunities.

Students' class ranks are determined by comparing their GPA to the GPA of peers in the same grade. So, if your student is a senior at a high school with 700 seniors, each of them will receive a number, 1-700. The person who has the highest GPA will be ranked #1.

Your student's class rank also determines his or her class percentile. If your student's school does not list his or her percentile, colleges may ask the student to figure it out.

Here is an easy way to figure out your student's class percentile:

1. Divide your student's class rank by the number of students in their grade.

2. Multiply by 100.

3. Subtract that number from 100.

For example, if there are 700 students in your student's grade, and he or she is ranked 105th, then your student is in the 85th percentile [because (105/800) 100=15, and 100-15=85].

Percentiles matter! Some states offer high school students guaranteed admission to state universities if they have a certain class rank.

More important class rank information to consider:

- Class rank can be weighted or un-weighted.

- Class rank is only one criterion that colleges use to determine your student's academic abilities.

- Some high schools no longer use class rank due to growing concerns that it causes students to take less challenging courses.

- Your student's class rank can typically be found on his or her high school transcript or report card.

- If your student's high school doesn't include class rank, it won't negatively affect their chances of getting into college.

- A desirable class ranking can also mean FREE money!

Application essay: This can be the "deal breaker!" If your student's essays do not match his or her high caliber GPA and test scores, the entire application will suffer.

Consider this situation: The application reader has several hundred applications to read. If every student has a perfect GPA and every student has a perfect SAT or ACT score, then the essay has the potential to be a powerful final decision maker.

The college application essay is like nothing your student has written before. High school English focuses on the mechanics of writing, not necessarily how to write the perfect college application essay.

It is important to note that for this essay, not all topics are good topics. A student's voice ought to authentically shine through, and the opening paragraph must hook the reader into continuing to read the essay.

Therefore, it is critical that two things must NOT happen when your student is writing their essay.

1) **Do NOT write the essay for them** (or pay a professional to do so). The application readers have seen it all, and they will be aware of unauthentic essays that are not the work of your student.

2) **Do NOT be your student's essay editor.** While it is difficult to back away from this step in the application process, as a parent, you are too close to the subject. You will not necessarily read your student's work with a critical eye. It is best to hire a professional essay editor who understands what colleges are looking for.

Remember: getting into college is very competitive, and I guarantee that your student is competing with other students who have access to everything they need to be successful. I know it is tempting to save a little money and ask the English teacher to edit the application, but beware: academic teachers are not always looking for the same things that the colleges are looking for.

A good College Consultant will offer essay editing as part of what they offer your student. It is worth its weight in gold, and it's one of the services I offer all of my clients!

You will also want to make sure that your student's essay adds to their application. Do not have your student just repeat the sports, activities, and leadership positions that take up the bulk of their application. A "slice of life" story that captures your student's personality and his or her core values can be very valuable. Adding something interesting like an anecdote or an activity they are especially passionate about can help students' college essay. These techniques can help the application reader get to know your student on a different level.

Below is a tool your student can use to get going on an essay plan:

Essay Brainstorming

Circle the words that best describe you and add your own:

Available	Innovative	Add Your Own
Accepting	Inspiring	
Active	Intelligent	
Adaptable	Introverted	
Aggressive	Intuitive	
Ambitious	Kind	
Appreciative	Mature	
Analytical	Nervous	
Arrogant	Original	
Articulate	Optimist	
Assuming	Passive	
Direct	Parental	
Diplomatic	Perfectionist	
Disciplined	Persuasive	
Driven	Playful	
Effective	Respectful	
Efficient	Rowdy	
Energetic	Sassy	
Frantic	Sarcastic	
Fearful	Scientific	
Family	Self-reliant	
Giving	Sensible	
Happy	Sensitive	
Hurried	Sentimental	
Independent	Social	

Recommenders: Is your student well rounded and valued by their teachers, coaches, or people in your community? Picking the best recommenders is very important to the application.

Before your student jumps to ask just anybody to write a recommendation letter, consider how the recommender writes. Is the coach a great writer? Will a particular teacher be able to offer the "real you" to colleges? If your student is not sure whether to ask someone to recommend him or her, then that candidate is probably not the correct person.

Your student's recommenders should know your student by name if they pass them in the hall. The recommender should know what kind of person your student is. Ideally, a recommender should have a story to tell about the student. The best recommenders tend to be English, Math, Science, History, or Language teachers.

There is a strategy on how your student should pick the recommenders, and they will want to make sure to ask at least three teachers if they would be willing to write a letter of recommendation. This is not the time to surprise a teacher who does not know them well.

Interview: If your student gets the opportunity to be interviewed by one of his or her potential colleges, what is a good next step? If your student can speak well to teachers and adults in general, then I recommend that he or she interview with the school if it is feasible for your family's budget.

Preparing for the interview must not be overlooked. What your student wears, the questions they ask, and how they represent themselves is very important. Again, colleges are looking for similarities. Does the student match his or her GPA, test scores, essay etc.? Is there anything that stands out about your student? If your student is confident in himself or herself, this can be a huge win!

The interviewer will write up a report and send it back to the application reviewing team. The interview not only shows the college that your student is interested; it also confirms that the student would be a great match for the college.

I spend a whole day preparing my student to know what to expect and all the do's and don'ts in preparation for the interview.

Extracurricular Activities: When it comes to applying to colleges, it is no longer viable to just be an academic student. Colleges and universities are looking for well-rounded and balanced students. Going to school, studying, and gaming on the TV do not amount to an impressive college resume.

Here are many questions to consider regarding your student's extracurriculars':

- Does your student have a theme that captures all of the activities that they enjoy, or are they all over the place?

- Have they stayed with the same activities throughout high school, or have they hopped around inconsistently?

- When your student is not in school, what are they doing?

- Is your student shopping, at the beach, hanging out with friends, watching TV, playing on the computer, spending time on social media and their phone? (Beware: Those are all red flags! Point your student in a direction with more focused passions.)

- Does your student participate in clubs, sports, or organizations?

- How much time are they spending at these events outside of school?

- Is your student using his or her free time to help others?

- Is your student working on being a productive citizen?

- Have they started or led a club?

Colleges want to know everything about your student and their free time will tell them a lot about the student/leader they are.

Extra-Curricular Activities

Activity Name   completed: 9th 10th 11th 12th

Hours per week
Weeks per year
Leadership

Activity Name   completed: 9th 10th 11th 12th

Hours per week
Weeks per year
Leadership

Activity Name   completed: 9th 10th 11th 12th

Hours per week
Weeks per year
Leadership

Activity Name   completed: 9th 10th 11th 12th

Hours per week
Weeks per year
Leadership

Passion/Talent: Teenagers can be complex creatures, and it is really important at this time in their lives to discover and to decide what they are passionate about. When it comes to college applications, it is time to ask the student: What have you done with your passion?

If you asked your student to list 10 things they are passionate about, and if they only had 5 minutes, could they do it? What would you list if I asked you to write down 10 things your student is passionate about?

Loving what your he or she does with his or her own free time will go a long way in helping colleges see the kind of student your child will be if accepted into their college. Colleges are looking for students with passion! They are not looking for a student to come

61

to their college and just take away an academic education. The goal is that your student will be a dynamic and active presence on their campus, one that will lead others to find their passion and success.

Athletes and students in the band have a slight advantage with this question. In most cases, it is obvious that a student athlete has passion for his or her particular sport and that they work hard to perfect their skills. Students in music or band must practice long hours and show passion for their talent.

Dedication and determination tell a lot about your students. Activities must be meaningful to them, but their passion should also be an integral part of their high school experiences.

What makes your student unique: What sets your student apart from all the other candidates? How will your student be remembered?

Your student will most likely have to answer questions like, "*What makes you unique?" or "Tell me something that I cannot read in your application."* How would your student answer this question? Do they have something about them that will make them a better candidate than another student? How will they stand out from the other tens of thousands of students that are applying to the same school? If they begin their planning process early enough, there should be plenty of time for a student to pursue at least one meaningful activity about which he or she is passionate.

Geography: Where do you live, and why do you want to attend the college to which you are applying (especially if the school is not in your state)?

What colleges want to know from your student is:

- Why our school?

- Why do you want to leave your friends and family?

- Is your student running from something or to something?

- Are you willing to pay out-of-state tuition if your student is accepted?

In some cases, going across the country for college tells the application editor that the student is confident and mature.

Community Service: What have you done for someone else that did not benefit you? Is your student a caring and compassionate person?

A quick anecdote: While I sat down to write this chapter, I was approached by a 9-year-old who offered me some lemonade. She went on to tell me that she was collecting donations for the Make-a-Wish charity. In the process of serving me lemonade, my new friend explained why she is raising money. She told me that during her flag day at school, someone came and told her school that the Make-A-Wish foundation gives kids their last wish. She told me that all the money she raised was going to help someone she never met do something very special. The passion that my new friend showed at 9-years old will take her far in life.

The goal of a community service project should be to do something your student is passionate about. Not all community service hours are created equal. I will share with you two examples to demonstrate the difference.

COLLEGE READY CASE STUDY: COMMUNITY SERVICE

STUDENT 1

I have one student that I will call Trevor who hired me the fall of his Senior year in high school. He had a 4.59 GPA and solid test scores. However, he only had 40 hours of community service (which he needed to graduate from his high school). His hours came from a random assortment of projects like dog washing, car washes, collecting canned goods, etc. None of these service hours were bad, BUT they just did not show one clear picture of Trevor's passion.

He would show up, do his time, and then he would just leave. For Trevor, service was more about checking off a list of hours than actually enjoying the act of service.

STUDENT 2

My second student, whom I will call Molly, started my strategy program the summer of her 8th grade year. She was passionate about helping others, however she could not figure out what she wanted to do for her service project. Her brother had gone to Africa that summer to volunteer at an orphanage in Kenya, and his stories had touched her heart. However, for Molly, the photos of the children without clothing made her tear up every time she looked at them.

After spending some time getting to know Molly and assessing her passions, we came up with the perfect community service project. She would make a project to help clothe a group of children who could not afford clothing. Molly decided that she wanted to provide shoes to the Kenyan children her brother had spent time with. She started small, and soon invited her three closest friends to get involved. They chose to do a shoe drive, and they went out into their community to collect shoes. The group made drop off boxes, signs, and fliers for distribution in their local community and in their high school.

To their surprise, the girls collected 10 large trash bags of gently used shoes. The group was so excited that they spent much of their free time sorting the shoes and packing them in boxes. At the end of the week, they took the boxes to the post office feeling a huge sense of accomplishment. But they hit a road block when the boxes were weighed: the total for shipping would cost more than $400.00. They did not have that kind of money, so they packed up their boxes of shoes and took them home, feeling deflated. That's when Molly showed her true leadership and rallied her group for an alternative plan.

The group worked together to find local children in need of shoes. By the end of the following week, the shoes were delivered to a local charity that delivered donated clothing to families who were homeless. The tenacity this group showed was amazing, but the rest of their story is even better!

Family and friends had shared Molly's story, and people were coming out of the woodwork to volunteer with her group. I suggested that it was time for Molly to come up with a name for her organization, and she choose "Dress of Hope." This was the beginning of Molly's dream come true. Her group had now grown to three high schools. Instead of shipping heavy shoes, Molly decided they would turn gently used pillowcases into little dresses and ship them all over the world to children in need of clothing. Molly and her group had never sewn anything before so I gave them a basic sewing lesson.

Their project was off and running. While some of the group continued to make dresses, others got on social media and created hype about what they were doing. A website was built, and they had a page on every form of social media.

Through this community awareness, a doctor heard about the project. She was very active in the organization "Doctors Without Borders," and she arranged for doctors to hand-deliver the dresses to children in need. By this point, two more schools had joined the group, helping to make dresses by the dozens. By Molly's junior year, dresses had been delivered to 23 different countries. Hundreds of children were wearing their pretty new dresses with smiles on their faces.

Up until this time Molly had not delivered one dress directly to children in need. Her dream was to go to a country and work in an orphanage just like her brother had. Molly's family could not afford this kind of trip, so Molly got creative and did fundraisers for money and awareness.

By the summer before her senior year, Molly was on her way to Peru to work in an orphanage and deliver her final batch of dresses. The looks on the little girls' faces when they received a pretty dress made by Molly were priceless. This is an example of how even local acts of service can grow to great global acts of charity.

This is an example of one of my students Community Service projects:

Everyone wants to make a difference, but not everyone can. Dress of Hope is an organization that was designed to cloth kids throughout our World. Kids throughout each country go each day wearing a shirt they find in a trashcan, or no clothes at all. We want to help change this. Our goal is to sew enough dresses to make an impact in other countries. We wish to make EVERY child feel loved.

Imagine a World where every little girl owned a dress.

I share both stores so you may see that a service project with passion means so much more than checking off service hours. Molly graduated with over 1,300 service hours and was rewarded with several scholarships. The essay written for her college application evoked so many emotions. Molly got into every college she applied to, except for one.

More importantly, doing something nice for others gave Molly so much more than she ever expected. Molly is now a freshman in her dream college majoring in Nursing and loving her college experience.

A community service project led by your student shows colleges that they have passion, leadership, organization skills, tenacity, the ability to think outside of the norm, and so much more. This project will share another side of your student's story. Your student's GPA, test scores, and activities will only tell a small portion of who they really are. The service project sets each student apart and has the power to bring an application to life.

Community Service

Activity Name   completed: 9th 10th 11th 12th

Hours per week
Weeks per year
Leadership

Activity Name   completed: 9th 10th 11th 12th

Hours per week
Weeks per year
Leadership

Activity Name   completed: 9th 10th 11th 12th

Hours per week
Weeks per year
Leadership

Activity Name   completed: 9th 10th 11th 12th

Hours per week
Weeks per year
Leadership

Leadership: When you think of the word "Leader," what is the first thing that comes to your mind? Maybe it is structured leadership at school like the Associated Student Body (ASB). Maybe it is the Drum Major or Conductor of the school's band. What about the captain of your student's sport team? Boy scouts or Girl scouts often come to mind, especially if the student has achieved the Eagle or Gold award.

Some students may find their leadership in a club or service project. The list of Leadership opportunities is long and varied. Do you know what type of Leadership is the most impressive to colleges? It is the student who rises up to lead in the same organization over time. It is the student who comes up with a need in their community and leads others to provide help. It is a student who can lead people who are older, younger, or even the same age. It is one who can organize and lead a group to accomplish their goal. It is students who may captain their soccer team to victory while teaching younger students how follow their dreams of someday competing in their sport.

Getting accepted into college is not an easy process. With the proper plans and knowledge, it can be accomplished without losing your mind. Many parents save for college but will not hire a tutor, test prep instruction, or a college planner. I suggest, getting the tutor if needed, hire a great test prep company, and seek the help of a knowledgeable college planner. By seeking help from experts, your student will have a much better chance of getting into the college of his or her dreams and earning merit money!

When your student completes their college applications, I recommend that you or a professional review the application before they click the submit button. Consider the checklist below:

- ✓ Log into the application.
- ✓ Keep all login passwords in a safe, easily accessible place.
- ✓ Make a note of the regular decision deadline.
- ✓ Make a note of the early decision deadline.
- ✓ Request high school transcript sent.
- ✓ Request midyear grade report sent.
- ✓ Find out if an admission test is required.
- ✓ Take an admission test, if required.
- ✓ Take other required or recommended tests.
- ✓ Send admission test scores.
- ✓ Send other test scores.
- ✓ Request recommendation letters.
- ✓ Send thank-you notes to recommendation writers.
- ✓ Draft initial essay.
- ✓ Proofread essay for spelling and grammar.

- ✓ Have your essay edited twice.
- ✓ Revise your essay.
- ✓ Proofread your revised essay, checking for word count.
- ✓ Interview at college campus.
- ✓ Have an alumni interview.
- ✓ Submit FAFSA.
- ✓ Submit PROFILE if needed.
- ✓ Make a note of the priority financial aid deadline.
- ✓ Make a note of the regular financial aid deadline.
- ✓ Complete college application.
- ✓ Make copies of all application materials.
- ✓ Pay application fee.
- ✓ Sign and send application.
- ✓ Submit college aid form, if needed.
- ✓ Submit state aid form, if needed.
- ✓ Confirm receipt of application materials.
- ✓ Send additional material, if needed.
- ✓ Tell your school counselor that you have applied.
- ✓ Receive letter from office of admission.
- ✓ Receive financial aid award letter.
- ✓ Meet deadline to accept admission and send deposit.
- ✓ Accept financial aid offer.
- ✓ Notify the colleges you will not be attending.

CHAPTER 5

Affordability: Can Your Family Afford College? Can Your Student Afford Not To Go To College?

The biggest question families have is: "Can our family afford college"?

The answer is a resounding, "YES." But there is one caveat, and that caveat is: Your student can afford to go to college, **BUT** only if the cost of college is planned properly.

The biggest setback that can prevent anyone from obtaining a college degree is the large financial cost of attending. While it is true that attending college may be one of the largest expenses your family will ever face, the importance of a college education has become evident in terms of earning potential within today's economy.

These questions hit home for me personally. Neither of my parents received a college degree, and I watched them work day and night to make a good living for our family. Back in the day, you could make it without a college degree as long as you had a lot of ambition and a strong work ethic.

My mom was a hairdresser and owned several beauty salons; she made a lot of money doing what she loved to do. My dad is an entrepreneur at heart and has started and owned several businesses and real estate investments. He lives a comfortable life and enjoys his leisure time and traveling.

Growing up, my dad would mention that he thought college was important for my future, but he did not tell me how to get into college. My mother thought college was not necessary, and she believed that I should get a job right out of high school like she did. Both of my parents were loving and supportive, but I grew up unsure whether college would be the right decision for me. My parents were doing fine without the extra four years of school or debt. Because I had no idea what I wanted to do after high school, I thought I would give college a try.

I am so glad that I did. What I experienced was more than just a great education!

Here are some of the life lessons I learned in college:

- ✓ I learned how to live with a roommate whom I had never met.

- ✓ I learned how to care for myself (what today's kids call "adulting" – cooking, washing clothes, cleaning, making doctor's appointments, etc).

- ✓ I gained confidence each year that I attended college and fought for each and every one of my grades.

- ✓ I learned that if I did not go and seek a job, it would not come to me.

- ✓ I learned that students from all over the world could be your friends.

- ✓ I learned for the first time how to balance a budget, balance a checkbook, and balance life!

- ✓ After changing my major 5 times, I learned that without proper planning, a 4-year degree could take 5 years. (Thank goodness for summer school and winter session!)

The reason I included this chapter is because if you, as the parent, do not see the value in a college education, your student will not either. Many parents like mine were not sure what college was all about, so they left the planning up to their students. This lack of planning and parent involvement can cost your student time and money.

Consider this: would you allow your 18-year-old to buy a home for you without your knowledge or input? Would you allow your 18-year-old to buy a car with a loan they had no idea how to pay back? College is an important life choice, and your student needs your help or the help of a professional.

If you are hoping that your student will have a better life than you did, encourage your student to attend college. Cost should not be the main factor when trying to decide if college is worth attending. The cost of college is just one key component to consider.

8 Ways to Assure That Your Student Gets An Affordable College Degree

1) Encourage your student to take the most challenging classes they can get an A in. Strong grades = merit scholarships.

2) Make sure your student has a strategic testing plan. There is nothing more important to financial freedom than strong test scores.

3) Encourage your student to test prep and score well on the PSAT. If your student scores well enough on the PSAT and becomes a National Merit finalist, he or she will be offered many options and scholarships.

4) If your student has the opportunity to take AP, Honors, IB or Dual enrollment classes, AND can earn strong grades, do it! The savings of taking theses classes in high school vs. college will save you thousands of dollars.

5) Have a strategy or plan as to which colleges your student will apply. In-State schools will offer different financial awards than out-of-state schools. A private school typically has more

money to offer than a state school. Applying to colleges where your student will graduate at the top of their class will give them many more financial opportunities.

6) Plan your college search by using the proper tools. Do not just rely on a broad search.

7) Look for colleges with strong financial packages and a track record of graduating in four years. Each additional year your student must stay in college is not only costing them time and the additional cost of college, but it is also taking away from their long- term income and retirement. (Do you know that there are 8 colleges where students can attend for FREE! If you are curious and would like to know the 8 colleges, contact College Ready. I am happy to share the list with you.)

8) Leverage your financial awards. If your student is not offered a financial aid award, use what other colleges have offered and appeal.

These are just a few ways to help with the rising cost of college.

Remember this: What you do not know, will cost you.

If you go on the Internet and research "College grads are landing most of the jobs in the recovery", you will see some alarming statistics. Not attending any college will have a negative effect on the financial future of most students.

It is fair to say that college is not for everyone. As a professional college consultant, I have turned down working with students who lack desire. If your student dislikes school, learning, teachers, time in the classroom, etc. then it is possible that your student maybe better served by enrolling them in a vocational school or trade school. With that said, most students would benefit by attending at least some college.

COLLEGE READY CASE STUDY: Affordability

I would like to share two students' stories after graduating from high school.

Student #1: The first student I will call Matt. Matt did not like anything about high school. He thought school was a waste of time, and he just wanted to graduate so he could get a job and make money. He had been working as a busboy at a local restaurant while attending high school. He was saving to buy a new car. Matt was an average student in high school, but he knew he did not want to attend college. He loved to work on his car and enjoyed building things. Matt's parents came to me with heavy hearts, worried about their son's future. After spending an hour with Matt, it was apparent the Matt wanted nothing to do with "more school."

We discussed his other options like attending a trade school or taking some classes at a community college. I will never forget the look on Matt's face when his father told him, "If you do not go to college, you will have to move out of our house and make it on your own!" Matt acted tough, like he did not care and like he would be happy to move out. Matt's mom, on the other hand, started to cry.

Student #2: The second student I will call Valerie. Valerie was a good student in English, History and loved taking Art classes. She was a strong student in those subjects, but she got poor grades in Math and Science. Valerie had never been on a college campus, and the thought of going away to school scared her. Her parents contacted me to request that I meet with her and offer guidance.

After about an hour, it became apparent that Valerie knew what SHE wanted to do, but she was scared to tell her parents. Valerie's dad wanted her to be practical and get a business degree. Valerie's mom wanted her to follow her passion and be an artist. What both parents did not know is that Valerie wanted to be a fashion designer or an interior designer. She wanted to own her own business and use her passion for art. The smiles on her parents' faces, were from ear to ear when Valerie was able to explain in a college counseling session just what she wanted to do in college. Her parents were so relieved that their daughter had a passionate plan for her education and that she did want to pursue a college degree.

Case Study Fast-Forward Five Years:

Matt decided he was tired of being told what to do, so he moved out of his parents' home and rented a room at a friend's house. He has a full-time job waiting tables, and he just started taking college classes. Unfortunately, all of Matt's friends have recently graduated from college and are starting their careers. They are buying new cars and have the luxury of going out to dinner and traveling. Matt now tells his story with regret and feels left behind.

Valerie, on the other hand, has graduated from college as a marketing major and started a job working for a clothing designer she has admired for years. She gets to employ her talents in design and set up advertising photo shoots. She lives in a decent apartment at the beach with her best friend, and she just purchased a new car. Valerie enjoys her career and looks forward to designing a clothing line of her own someday.

I do not tell these stories to stereotype or speak badly of either student. I share these stories to show how each student has their own path. Even siblings will not take the same path as another family member. There is no way to predict if going to college will make one student more successful than another.

What getting a college degree *will do* is give your student options. The more options you have in life, the better you will do!

A student with a college degree will always have his or her degree to fall back on and use for job applications. They will not be denied a job because they did not get a college education. Personally, I believe that knowledge is power and confidence. I have always taught my children to live life without regret.

Making a decision at 18 to not attend college may turn out to be a regret later. The same can be true about letting your 18-year-old take on student loans with no idea as to how he or she will pay them back. High school graduation is an absolutely pivotal time! Planning will save your student from regret and debt.

The Economy and its Effects on Education

Economics and recession also play an important part when planning to attend or not attend college. Going to college does not mean your student will not be affected by the recession, but it does mean that he or she will have a better chance of getting one of the few jobs available in their field during an economic downturn.

There are many students and families considering the value of a college education when debt and unemployment are soaring out of control based on media reviews. You will see in the graph below, with information compiled by the Pew Research Center, that college graduates ages 25-32 who are working full time earn $17,500 more than young adults having only a high school diploma. This same group has lower unemployment rates, as well as fewer students living at the poverty level.

Annual Earnings ...

(median among full-time workers, in 2012 dollars)

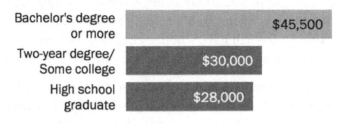

Bachelor's degree or more — $45,500
Two-year degree/ Some college — $30,000
High school graduate — $28,000

Unemployment Rate ...

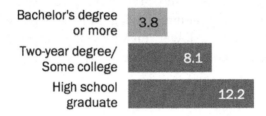

Bachelor's degree or more — 3.8
Two-year degree/ Some college — 8.1
High school graduate — 12.2

And Share Living in Poverty ...

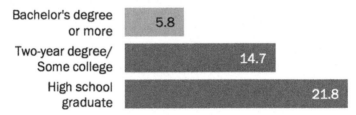

Bachelor's degree or more — 5.8
Two-year degree/ Some college — 14.7
High school graduate — 21.8

Notes: Median annual earnings are based on earnings and work status during the calendar year prior to interview and limited to 25- to 32-year-olds who worked full time during the previous calendar year and reported positive earnings. "Full time" refers to those who usually worked at least 35 hours a week last year. The unemployment rate refers to the share of the labor force (those working or actively seeking work) who are not employed. Poverty is based on the respondent's family income in the calendar year preceding the survey.

Source: Pew Research Center tabulations of the 2013 March Current Population Survey (CPS) Integrated Public Use Micro Sample

PEW RESEARCH CENTER

The numbers don't lie. When it comes to making money, statistics are in favor of a college education. When considering if the cost of college is worth it, I often get many questions like the following:

1. **My student does not know what they want to do or major in; is community college a better option?** –My reply: A better option than what? Not going to college at all? Taking a gap year and starting college after the gap year? Staying at a community college and then transferring to a four-year college? The answer to the question is not a yes or a no. The answer is that it depends on the individual student's wants and desires. Statistically, having some college is better than none and a four-year college degree is optimal for a favorable financial future.

2. **Are Ivy League schools the best option?** My answer: NO. Ivy League schools are not the best option for all students. If a student is fortunate enough to be accepted into an Ivy school, they will be competing with the best of the best. The pressure may be too much for many students, and it can also be very difficult socially. Each student must work at his or her own plan. Success is not the name of a school, it's what the student does with an education.

3. **Is a more expensive college going to ensure that my student gets a better job when they graduate?** The truth: There are no guarantees that any college can promise your student a better job than another college. With that said, colleges with a strong alumni network can be beneficial when looking for a job.

4. **What if the career my student has chosen to pursue will not make enough to cover their college debt?** This is a good question, as it is always best to start with the end in mind. If your student wants to enter a career that only makes $40,000 a year, it does not make sense to get a student loan for $50,000 a year. Planning is critical here! The student should be advised to pick a college that is less expensive or one that he or she will be able to attend for free or a reduced rate.

5. **You may even be asking yourself: Why should I send my student to college if I have done fine without a college degree?** I advise you to consider your student's potential future. Opportunity is the key reason to encourage your student to attend college. Now with more students than ever getting a college degree, it is critical to be competitive. The U.S. is no longer just a manufacturing economy. The U.S. economy is now based on knowledge and technology. The importance of a college education now can be compared to a high school education 30 years ago. *College is the bridge to opportunities in the future.*

There are additional benefits of sending your student to college. Consider things that cannot be quantified such as exposure to books, lectures, stimulating conversations, building relationships, and thinking outside the proverbial bubble. All of these experiences allow for additional growth and development, which provides a competitive edge in the job market.

Also, consider the connections your students will make with their teachers, other students, and alumni. The more connections your student has when he or she graduates, the more opportunities there will be for securing a great job right out of college. Lastly, having a college degree often leads to greater promotion, more expansive opportunities, and higher salaries.

The bottom line: Attending college provides students with knowledge and the experience they are no longer able to get from a secondary education. With proper planning, your student can get a college degree without going into debt. Every piece of research I found documented the benefits of having a college degree. If the cost is no longer the reason "why not," I would encourage your student to at least give college a try.

If you are unsure if your student should attend college, give us a call. College Ready can help you with an assessment that will help you decide if college is a good match for your student.

CHAPTER 6

Decisions: What Happens If Your Student Does Not Pick The Right College

Question: Do you know how much it will cost you if you pick the wrong college?

Answer: A lot! Time, money and energy.

Deciding which college is the best for your student: As a parent, this can be one of the most frustrating stages of the college planning process. When you ask your student, "What is your dream school?" or "Where do you want to go to college?" – the answer will often be, "I don't know!"

This is not uncommon. Your student is most likely a little nervous to pick the wrong school. So, how do you help your student pick the college that is the best fit for your student? Each college and university is just as unique as your student is. Your student will want to pick a college based on his or her personal and career interests, career goals, past academic success, and test records.

Parents often want to know: where and how they can get assistance for the daunting task of finding the right school. Below are some options for you and your student:

- ✓ Meet with the high school counselor.

- ✓ Buy a book about college selection at the bookstore.

- ✓ Attend college open houses.

- ✓ Research colleges on the Internet.

- ✓ Contact each college, and speak with the admissions department.

- ✓ Ask a neighbor or friend with experience to help you.

- ✓ Hire an Independent College Consultant (Not an Insurance Agent or Financial Planner). Make sure it's someone who specializes in finding the perfect College Match.

What you do *NOT* want your student to do:

Pick A College Based on Its Identity as a Top Ranked College.

Caution! Colleges can inflate their rankings. Consider this: if a college sends out letters of interest to thousands of under-qualified students who then apply to that college that they are NOT a fit for, the acceptance rate for that college is inflated. The lower the acceptance rates, the higher that college is ranked. You may be feeling frustrated that you are not sure what information you can trust online or which college rankings are legit.

Buyer beware: College is a money-making business, and many schools will do everything they can to persuade your student to apply to their college. Do not believe everything you read. It is important to know the graduation rate for a student to graduate in 4 years at each college your student is considering. Research the value of the degree and major your student is considering. Know what internships and job opportunities are available upon graduation. Ask what financial aid is awarded and to what percentage of students.

When I help my students start the college matching process, these are four primary things to consider:

1. **I assure all of my students that there is a perfect college for them.** The thing is: they may not even know the name of the school yet. There are perfect matches for 5.0 students as well as average students; they just need to know where to find these schools.

2. **I assure all my students that the college picking process does not need to be stressful.** So much stress comes from the fear of the unknown and the misinformation they receive from friends. Knowledge is power.

3. **I help my student's change their focus of, "The best college" to the "Perfect College" for that particular student.** From size to geographic location to campus culture to academic caliber, colleges can vary as widely as the students applying to them!

4. **I explain that there is a sequence of steps that will need to be followed for success.** I always start with the end in mind. For example: What does the student want to do for a career? Most students will not have any idea how to answer this question. Going through a series of assessments is just a starting point. Finding a student's passion is the most critical piece to finding out what will make them happy now and in the future.

For many students, choosing a college is their first major decision. Going through this process will provide lifelong skills such as: taking initiative, making decisions, showing tenacity, and being responsible. With guidance, this process can be exciting and enjoyable. The end result can be powerful: graduating from a college in four years and having a job waiting for the student after graduation.

For Parents: Try to remember that you had your chance at a college choice, and that this time around, it is your student's turn to pick the college that he or she wants. You can assist your student by encouraging him or her to go step-by-step through the process. Help your student take the planning process seriously.

Encourage them to think, reflect, research, and choose carefully. Remind your student that the process will take time; it cannot be accomplished in a day. I recommend setting aside an hour a week to discuss the process and how they are feeling and progressing.

Throughout the process, try to encourage and support your student's research skills. Ask open-ended questions that can't be answered with a short yes or no. Set your expectations upfront with timing and next steps. All the while, keep in mind that the student's GPA must come first. Without a solid GPA, there would not be a need for the college search.

For Students: You have worked very hard to be able to make the decision of which college to choose. Do not rush through the process; instead take your time. Know that you will be living at your college for at least four years. Consider the location, the size of the school, and all the elements that are important to you.

This process can be intimidating. There are no rights or wrongs, just choices to make.

If this process seems overwhelming, I recommend that you seek help from an experienced college counselor like myself. You can go to my website and book a FREE discovery call with me! A competent and experienced counselor can bring clarity to this process. Be careful not to listen solely to friends or well-meaning adults.

College is a choice, and big decisions can be difficult for a teenager or young adult. Picking a college is an important choice that will lead to success in the future. If your student invests time and energy into the college search, he or she will find many colleges in which to choose from. If your student chooses not to seek information, but takes the "wait and see approach" to college selection, he or she will most likely be disappointed with his or her final college options.

Your student's first decision is whether he or she has a desire to attend college. If the answer is YES, then I suggest the student make a list of the outcomes they desire from a college education. Simply stated, the student needs to write down or verbalize exactly why they want to go to college. If the student still isn't sure, you can count on him or her not following the steps to find the best-fit college.

Your student's second decision should be when to start school. Does the student want to take a Gap-year or jump right in after high school? The Gap year has become increasingly popular for a student who needs a break or wants to travel before pursuing further education.

Choosing a college should not be a stressful or a traumatic event. Your student may look at this process as positive and exciting or negative and overwhelming. The better they are informed about choices, the less stressful this process will be. If your student follows these simple steps, he or she will feel more in control of the situation.

- ✓ First, they need to analyze themselves as a student.
- ✓ Second, have them review the qualities that will make a college right for them.
- ✓ Third, use all the resources listed above to select the colleges to which they will apply.
- ✓ Lastly, after receiving all their acceptances, your student will get to pick which college is the best fit.

Misinformation can lead to a bad college match. Here's a list of common misperceptions to consider when selecting a college:

1. **Misperception:** A good college is difficult to get into.
2. **Truth:** There are thousands of great colleges for every kind of student.

    Misperception: The kids that get into the best schools have some secret skill that my student does not have.
3. **Truth:** Every student has individual gifts and talents; try not to compare your student to peers.

    Misperception: If your student has no idea what to be when he or she grows up, your student is not ready for college.

4. **Truth:** At least half of my students had no idea what they wanted to do after college until we started working together. It is normal for high school students not to know what they want to do. Do not let that hold them back from applying to college.

   Misperception: If your student does not get into college X, you have failed as a parent.

5. **Truth:** This is not true! The brand name of a college does not equal success or failure.

   Misperception: Picking a college because it is on some "best list" in a magazine is NOT a good strategy.

6. **Truth:** A good strategy is doing your own research or seeking out the help of a professional (an expert) that will help guide you to the best fit for your student.

   Misperception: There is a perfect college for every student.

7. **Truth:** Believing that there is only one perfect college for your student is setting your family up for a lot of heartache. If planned properly, there will be a perfect college match.

   Misperception: Good schools cost a lot of money.

8. **Truth:** You do not need to pay more money to get a better education. If your student's best match college costs less than other colleges, you should be celebrating.

   Misperception: The cost of a college should be the main quality to consider.

9. **Truth:** There are eight colleges that offer free tuition in trade for working at the school. A four-year degree from one of these colleges will not cost anything. Knowledge is the key to success.

   Misperception: A student has to fit in a perfect student mold to be accepted.

10. **Truth:** Colleges consider many things when deciding who to admit to their college. They look at course selection,

grades, test scores, extracurricular activities, where the student went to high school, athletics etc.

Misperception: Be careful not to fall into the trap, "EVERYONE thinks that college X is the best" so that is where I want my student to attend.

11. **Truth:** With the right preparation, your student will find a school that is just the right fit!

COMMON PARENT QUESTIONS ABOUT COLLEGE

Where do you start when looking for the best match school for your student?

First, you will want to start the process by helping the student get to know himself or herself. Have your student consider the following questions:

- ✓ Is he or she ready to leave home?
- ✓ What are your student's greatest strengths?
- ✓ What are your student's areas of opportunity?
- ✓ What will colleges remember about your student after reading his or her application?

Sometimes, parents do not like what they learn about their students, and that can be a difficult conversation to have. Your student may have come to the conclusion that he or she does not have what it takes to get into the dream college; that reality is hard to swallow. The thought of leaving home can cause some students to become clingy to or distant from their parents. The thought of the unknown may be exciting to some students, yet very scary to others. The most important things that come from this self-assessment is that your student will start to formulate which type of college environment will help them thrive as a student and citizen.

Second, your student will need to decide what he or she is looking for in a college.

Your student will need to consider: size, location, admission possibilities, majors offered, costs, financial aid, diversity, sports, religion, student life, alumni support, time it takes to graduate, percentage of students who graduate with a job, and professors/class ratios. Students will need to consider whether they see themselves living at a school for four years without family.

Third, it's now time to have your student build their college list.

- ✓ Which colleges will your student consider?
- ✓ Which colleges will he or she apply to, and why?
- ✓ What would be their top pick perfect match college?

Doing this without the help of a professional can be very difficult. You may rely on your college visits, research you have done, or your high school counselor's help. Another option is to hire a college planner to help you with this process. Deciding which colleges to apply to is critical to your student's success. It will take time, patience, research skills, and a lot of determination.

There are some other things you will want your student to consider through this process:

1. Is the college being considered a reach, comfort, or safety college for your student?

2. Based on past acceptance stats, what are the chances of your student being accepted?

3. If your student is accepted, can you afford the college fees?

4. If you pick a college because they have your major, and then your student changes his or her major, will your student still feel as though the college is a perfect match?

5. If your student got into the college, would he or she really want to live there?

6. Will your student be happy at a religious college or at a school without religion?

7. If your student is an athlete, does he or she want to play in college at a D1, D2, D3, or a club team?

8. If your student gets accepted as a Scholar Athlete, will he or she get to live with non-athletes? Will athletes get to pick a major, or will the coach do it for them? Will your student athlete get to play or ride the bench?

9. If your student is a Merit Scholar, would she or he be happier being a big fish in a small school, or a small fish in a big school?

10. What is the reality of your student sticking with the chosen major all 4 years?

Carefully consider all of the information above. However, if cost is the biggest issue, do not overlook it. Look for colleges that will meet the financial need of your student or give a merit scholarship. Always start with the end in mind.

Focus on the Net Price, Not the Sticker Price

4 year public college example

 *less*  *equal*   *What you owe*

Sticker Price
The college's published
tuition and fees

**Gift Aid and
Tax Benefits**

Net Price

Fourth, campus visits are very important to this process.

You do NOT need to go tour every college on your "to apply" list, but when you are down to your final few acceptances, you will want to spend some time on those campuses. Campus visits come in many shapes and sizes. You can walk onto most college campus any day of the week without calling ahead. You can walk around on your own, or you can download a self-guided tour at most colleges.

You can go to the admissions office, and they will direct you on how to use their map for a self-guided tour. Or you can call ahead and make an appointment for an official tour with a student guide.

If you are very interested in a college, let them know by going to their campus and signing up for a tour or a meeting with the admissions office. Colleges want to know that they are important to you and that you have taken the time to come and visit.

COMMON COLLEGE QUESTIONS FROM STUDENTS:

- **When should I start to visit colleges?** Now, is always my answer! It is never too early for your student to see what they are working so hard for. You do not need to go out of state to see what is the difference between a public school, private school, liberal arts school, research school, large school, small school etc. Tour colleges near your home until your student has an idea about which kind college seems like the best fit.

- **Why should I tour a college?** There is nothing better than learning about what you like and do not like first hand. Your student should always spend time dining in the dining halls . Does your student see him or herself being happy there? Campus visits bring college to life.

- **Do I need to prepare for the college visit?** When you are in the research phase of the process, go online and look at key information like size, location, diversity, majors offered, what is the college best known for, what makes the college unique etc. Anything that matters to your student should be put on a check-off list, and initial thoughts should be recorded for future reference. After your student has been accepted to the colleges, he or she will want to learn everything possible about each college. Students will want to write out a list of pros and cons for each college visit. If prospective students can stay the night on campus in the dorms, I highly recommend it. If your student knows a student that is currently attending the college, reach out to them for a personal tour and perhaps an overnight visit.

- **Should I ask questions during the visit?** Your student will gain the most insight from a college by asking specific questions. Here are several great questions to get your student started:

  o How are roommates chosen?

  o What type of student seems happiest here?

  o What percent of your freshman class graduate from your college? In four years?

  o Are any of your majors impacted?

  o What happens if I pick a major and change my mind?

  o What is social life like at your college? Greek life, club sports, clubs, leadership etc.

  o What are weekends typically like during the school year?

  o What percentages of students commute from home?

  o Do you cap the number of credits a student is allowed to enroll in during a semester?

  o Do you use student teachers or professors to teach the classes?

- **Do I need to meet with the admissions department?** I always recommend at least stopping by the admissions department and asking to be added to the school's mailing list or interested students list. If you have the opportunity to sit down with an admissions officer, do it. The following questions, will help you get the communication started:

  o Will any of my high school classes like AP or IB count for college credit? Will I have to take a class if I passed the AP exam in the same subject?

  o If I get accepted as one major and decide I want to change it, will that be possible?

  o Will I be given the opportunity to have a Minor if I want to do the additional work?

- o If I sign up to take a class that is full, what are my options?

- o Do you offer study abroad programs? Semester? Year-long?

- o What Majors are impacted, and which are your most popular majors?

- o Do you help students find a job once they graduate?

- o How active is your Alumni group?

- o How many students are in your largest class? How many students in an average class?

- o Are there any tests I will need to take before I start college (subject tests etc.)?

- **Should my parents go on the college visit with me?** If you want them to or if they are paying, then the answer is "absolutely!" Parents may see something that you may overlook. Sometimes they know you better than yourself, and they may be able to add some reflection or a different point of view.

- **If I am given a chance for a personal interview, should I take it?** YES, unless you are shy and have a difficult time in an interview process. Here are a few sample questions your student may be asked: Why are you interested in this college? What do you enjoy doing when you are not in school? What is your favorite subject and least favorite subject? What other colleges are you considering?

The list can be long and varied, but the bottom line is that the admissions officer is writing down notes in your file like: Does this student match his or her application? Is he or she self-confident? Will this candidate be a good match for this college? What will this student contribute when he or she attends here? The admissions office is trying to assess if students are a good fit to be successful at a particular college. After the interview, always ask for a business card, and follow up with a handwritten thank you note.

- **How can I tell if the college is the best one for me?** Have your student keep a notebook for tours of all of their potential colleges. Have them list the following items and answer them for each college visit:
  - College name, location, date and who they spoke to
  - Likes and dislikes about the campus
  - Academic fit
  - Social fit
  - What stood out
  - Overall rating 1-10

There are so many more questions I practice with my students, and the way that admissions departments they receive answers is very important. Role-playing with your student will give him or her the confidence to sit down with the admissions department.

Fifth, use what you have learned on your campus tours and through your research to create an essay that will prove your student is the best candidate for this college.

Your student's essay can be the final decision that weighs in on whether he or she gets accepted or rejected. The essay is often used as the final determining factor if your students' application is similar to another student's. Sometimes, the admission reader needs to make a decision to admit just one. At some colleges, your student's essay will be read by two or three readers and a committee. Your student must look at his or her essay as a way to let colleges know who they are and what they are passionate about. Many colleges call the essay a "personal statement," and some say it is optional. To be clear, it is **never** truly optional. Your student should **always** provide the personal statement.

The college match process of helping your student with self-reflecting, figuring out what he or she is looking for in a college, building the college list, visiting college campuses, and creating the perfect essay should involve the entire family. Choosing a college is a big decision. It will most likely be one of the largest decisions your student will make in his or her lifetime.

The parents' role in this process will be as counselor, advisor, cheerleader, and accountability partner. If your student welcomes your advice, this can be a fun process that brings your family even closer. If your student only hears parent commands like: "Clean your room, do your chores, finish your homework, and write your essays," then this process can cause a lot of friction in the family.

Sometimes, hiring a professional College Planner can help with all facets of this process, including keeping the student and family happy.

What happens if you choose not to go through all the steps in this process? What happens if you *do* go through the steps recommended, and your student does not get accepted into a college he or she wants to attend or you can afford? What happens if your student accepts a college he or she thinks is perfect, just to find out that it is not a good match? What happens if you leave this entire process up to your student, and you do not like his or her final college choices?

The reality is that picking the wrong college for your student will cost them both time and money!

Most colleges will only let you apply during a short application window in the fall. If your student misses the application deadline, he or she will have to wait another year to apply. If your student starts at a college and later figures out is not a good fit, he or she can either apply to a college that has open enrollment, or wait a year to apply to another college. In the worst-case scenario, the student pays and takes a class at a college they do not wish to go back to. Then, not all the class credits will transfer to the new college. This will cost both time and money.

Many colleges will not consider your student to be a transfer student until he or she has earned 60 units. Transferring is not the best option for many reasons, but most importantly, it will cost your student time, money, and a lot of frustration. It is not easy moving away from home, making new friends, and getting comfortable in a new environment just to realize that the college is not a good fit.

Typically transfer students have to attend school for an extra year in order to receive a bachelor's degree that would have taken only 4 years to earn without transferring.

See below for the potential cost for a transferring student: Cost includes tuition, room and board, and other fees based on the average sticker price for an in-state public college. It does not include financial aid.

Cost of Transferring example

No Transfer
$25,125 × 4 years = $100,500

1 Transfer
$25,125 × 5 years = $125,625

2 Transfers
$25,125 × 6 years = $150,750

The lesson is: Planning and strategizing is the key to a strong college match that will lead to a wonderful college experience.

CHAPTER 7

Timeline For Success: What Should You And Your Student Do, And When Should You Do It?

Proper planning is the key to having options when applying to college. Having a strategy and knowing when to implement each stage is critical to your student's future.

Just showing up to high school and taking the classes necessary to graduate will not get a student into the college of his or her dreams. At best, going through high school without a plan will earn a student a diploma and possibly entrance into the local community college or state school.

There are many paths that students take in high school, and no two students are the same. My desire is to give you a general guideline as to what is the minimum your student must do to get into a four-year college.

COLLEGE READY CASE STUDY ON COURSE-WORK: EVERY CLASS COUNTS, AND IT *DOES* MATTER IN WHICH ORDER YOUR STUDENT TAKES EACH CLASS.

One of my students learned this lesson on courses the hard way. Justine and Keri were best friends and did everything together. Justine was a gifted student, and Keri was an average student. In 8th grade the high school counselor came to their middle school to tell them about high school and what they should expect.

Both girls were very excited to start high school, but neither had any idea about what high school classes to take. The high school counselor gave them general rules of what they must accomplish to graduate high school; however, neither of them received personal guidance.

Justine had always had straight A's and was invited to start high school in honors classes. Keri, on the other had had A's and B's, but was not accepted into any honors classes. Justine felt bad for Keri so she told her she would take regular classes with her so they could be in the same classes together. Keri felt much better knowing they would be together and that Justine could help her if high school would prove to be too difficult.

Neither of the girl's parents looked over their daughter's class schedules, and the girls had the freedom to choose whatever classes they wanted. On the very first day of school, Justine realized she had made a big mistake. The classes the girls chose together would be too easy and boring for her. Justine went to the high school counselor and waited in line to see if she could get her classes changed. When it was finally Justine's turn, she explained what had happened and asked the counselor if she could still be moved to the honors class she was offered at registration. He simply said "No" and told her it was too late; classes were full. Justine made the best of her freshman year and received all A's.

The following spring when Justine had the opportunity to select classes for her sophomore year, she was determined to make better choices. Unfortunately, Justine was never able to get placed in the honors or AP classes because she had been put on a different track. Not only did lack of planning hurt Justine's future, but it kept her from reaching her full academic potential.

SO, HOW DO YOU PREPARE YOUR STUDENT FOR FRESHMAN YEAR?

In middle school, if your student is invited to take a language, I suggest they take it. Have your student take the most challenging math they can be successful at learning. Teach your student study skills like where and when to study. If your student is struggling academically, hire a tutor as soon as possible. The classes your student takes in 8th grade will set the tone for their freshman year in high school. Many high schools will require that your student take a test to see if they are ready for an honors or AP class.

Freshman Year

- Teach your student how to get organized.

- Teach your student how to study.

- Utilize study groups.

- Let them explore their passions.

- Help your student set goals each semester, and make them measurable.

- This is the first year your student should take the PSAT.

- Have your student start his or her own community service project.

- Use the summer vacation and school year breaks wisely.

What to do Freshman year:

- **Teach your student how to prioritize.** Most students do more than just go to school. They have band practice, sports practices, community service, tutoring, and homework just to name a few activities. Unfortunately, high schools do not teach your student how to set priorities. Each class tells your student what must be done for that class. The problem is: every teacher thinks his or her class is the most important. Then in athletics, you have coaches telling students they need to practice more, to condition more, and to prepare to compete. The teenage to-do list is endless. Most students have no idea what to do, so they do the easiest things first. Usually they do not get to the difficult subjects.

If your student is lucky enough to be organized, he or she can usually get by without too much discomfort. For the other 90% of students who harbor habits like shoving homework into backpacks, losing books, not writing down assignments, and forgetting what to study for on a test, there will be consequences. Problems can escalate from small to huge very quickly.

As your student transitions from the hand-holding teachers in 8th grade to the reality of high school, I suggest you spend the first few weeks helping them to make a to do list. Teach your student how to prioritize tasks. Teaching your student this very important life skill early on will head off disaster down the road.

- **Teach your student how to get organized.** Start with a simple backpack and binder. If the teachers are specific on how to set up the binders, make sure your student has set it up properly the first time. Most of the time homework does not get turned in because the student can't find what they have completed. A planner of some sort is critical! There are many ways to get organized. Some examples for organization include: a day planner that you write in, Google calendar that syncs with your school calendar, phone notes, or computer notes.

The bottom line is that there are endless ways to get organized; your student just needs to find out what will work best for him or her. One of my students takes a photo of the classroom board at the end of every class and stores it on her cell phone to reference later.

- **Teach your student how to study.** If your student has always sat on the couch with the TV on and music playing, things will need to change. Establish a study desk in a quiet location with few distractions. Make sure the lighting is good and the chair is comfortable.

  Some students prefer to wear headphones and listen to music while they study. That is great, as long as they are getting their homework done and comprehending the material. It is always best to homework tasks with the subject that is the most difficult and end with the easiest subject. Study breaks are important, and healthy snacks are always helpful. Establish a "Social Media Free Zone".

  One of my parents says that she takes her son's cell phone and iPad and puts them in a drawer until his study break. Also, remember to turn off social media notifications on the computer that your student is working on. Learning how to study now will help your student be successful in college when you are not there to help them set up parameters.

- **Utilize study groups.** Encourage your student to invite classmates over to study as a group. They do not need to be all straight A students. The benefit of a study group is that each student is held accountable for doing their homework. Have each student go around the table and tell their answer. If they got the answer right, have them explain it to the students who did not get it correct. For the student who got the answer wrong, have them explain where they made their mistake. This kind of discussion is beneficial for all students. It holds them accountable for getting all their work done. No one likes to let friends down!

- **Let them explore their passions.** Your student's freshman year should be used as a time to explore their passions. For many freshmen, it is a time to find out what they are truly good at and what they enjoy doing the most.

Freshmen should try new clubs and organizations, challenge themselves with their classes, and see what they are really capable of accomplishing.

- **Help your student set goals each semester, and make them measurable.** What grade will your student achieve in each class? Try out for the JV team. Audition for the school play. Don't miss a day of school. Then at the end of the semester, revisit the goals to see how many of them your student accomplished.

- **This is the first year your student should take the PSAT.** Most schools will not announce that freshman can take the test. You will have to seek out the test information, but it is worth the effort.

- **Have your student start his or her own community service project.** I realize this may seem overwhelming, but it is possible. Every one of my students has completed their own service project and has benefited from it personally. These kinds of projects are also good college application material.

- **Use the summer vacation and school year breaks wisely**. If you do not plan your students summer, it will look something like this: Sleeping in late, going to the beach or mall, texting on the phone all day, playing video games or computer games, and stalking people on social media etc. You get the picture. Most students will not ask to wake up early and have a productive summer.

- Again, *planning* is the key to a great summer for your student. You may be asking yourself, "Great, but what does that *look like*?" Below are some great examples of what my students have done to make the best use of their summers and breaks:

  o Volunteer in another country.

  o Volunteer at a youth center.

  o Start or join community service projects.

- o Take a college class.
- o Learn CPR or First Aid.
- o Try a new sport or musical instrument.
- o Take an art class.
- o Do an internship.
- o Write a book.
- o Research and get work published.
- o Attend summer academic programs at colleges.
- o Join leadership camps.

I could write an entire chapter about great summer time activities. You should just be aware that in addition to school year activities and academics, colleges will ask how your student spent their time while *not* in school.

Sophomore Year

- Understand the PSAT and why it is important to take.
- Test preparation plan.
- What to do if your student is a procrastinator.
- Help your student find balance and manage their time.
- Community service should be growing and building momentum.
- Is leadership in your student's future?
- Expectations and dreams should be evaluated.
- Tour local colleges to compare and contrast
- Make summer plans.

What to do Sophomore year:

Picking the correct classes, at the best times, with the right teacher can be challenging, but with a strategic plan, it can be painless. The sophomore year is one of many changes and challenges. It is the first time that all students will take the PSAT. It is the first time your student will want to prepare for a test that they will not get a grade for. 10th grade is the year of test preparation and the first time for many students to have the ability to take their first AP class.

- Understanding what the PSAT is and why your student should have to take it may help alleviate any fears your student may be feeling. The PSAT is the practice test for the SAT test that will be used by colleges to assess your student's academic achievements. The PSAT asks similar questions as the SAT but does not have the writing section. The PSAT is also called the NMSQT (National Merit Scholarship Qualifying Test). I recommend reviewing the missed questions on the PSAT and learning from this practice test.

- Test preparation is not fun, and your student is not going to want to do it. There are many ways to prepare for the PSAT/SAT/ACT. The first thing you must consider is your student's learning style. Do they need to see it, hear it, write it, or all three for the information to be absorbed? Plan to have your student prepare for the test using that learning style. What I have found time and time again is that you will get what you pay for.

- What to do if your student is a procrastinator. This is a difficult personality trait to change, but you can show your student the benefits of doing work early or at least on time. I challenge my students to prepare for a test last minute and be aware of their stress. Then on the next test, I recommend having a study strategy and planned study timeline. After both tests have been completed, we meet to discuss what they learned. I have found that it is my smart, lazy students who procrastinate the most; they may get through high school easily, but they find it catches up with them in college.

- Help your student find balance and manage their time. I suggest to my students who need help in this area to write down everything they do for a week and the time they spend doing it. Next, we review the list and group the information into productive and nonproductive time. If the student is truly honest, they will see how much time they waste on social media and gaming. The following week, I suggest they approach the week with a strategy and plan how they will use their time on a calendar *"like a job that cannot be missed."* The students who really want to balance their lives and stop stressing out learn quickly that time management and planning is the key to a balanced life.

- Community service should be growing and building momentum. Help your student adjust his or her mission statement and adjust expectations. Is your student still passionate about the community service they chose? How can you adjust the current project to fit their changing needs? Make suggestions on how they can grow their project. Have your student reach out to friends at other high schools and their community so they can create a big event over summer break.

- Remember to keep track of all service hours and to have your student get them signed off on after the project has been completed. Do not wait until they are filling out their applications to try to remember where and when they did their community service.

- Since my company, College Ready, is a certifying organization for the President's Volunteer Service Award, all of my students who complete their service hours will receive a national service award based on their hours completed.

- Is leadership in your student's future? If the answer is yes, what will that look like? If the answer is, "I am not sure," it is time to strategize how your student can add leadership to their high school experience. Will they lead in their sport, school government, music, community service, clubs or organizations?

- Why is it important to start planning their sophomore year? If you wait until their junior year it may be too late to add to college applications. It is always a good idea to get your student involved with groups they will be able to lead in their junior and senior year. Solid leadership in well-known organizations will be important for your student's college application and help prepare your student for college and life. Leadership is important to colleges. Colleges are looking for well-rounded leaders to make a difference at their school. Colleges consider leaders to be mature, respected, passionate, and determined.

- Expectations and dreams should be evaluated and adjusted based on the rigor of classes and grades received your sophomore year. Time for a reality check to see if your student still has what it takes. Does your student still have the desire to continue on with the plan to attend his or her dream college? Did your student meet the goals that were set? This is not a time to be negative, but it is a good time to check in and see if adjustments need to be made.

- Tour local colleges to compare and contrast. This is a great year to take some local college tours. Pick a geographic location where you can see multiple schools in one or two days. Visit a large public college, a small private college, a state school, and a religious school (if one is being considered). Help your student understand what it will take to get into each college. Look at the average GPA, test scores, acceptance rate, community service hours needed, cost of attendance, years to graduate, job offers at graduation, financial aid and anything else that is important to your family.

- Does summer really matter? The answer is always going to be yes! This summer is a great time to explore what your student may want to major in when attending college. If they want to be an architect, suggest that your student seek out adults who are doing what they would like to do after college. If your student would like to be a doctor, suggest that your student volunteer at the local hospital or an orphanage and care for children or sick patients. If your student wants to go into computers, learning how to write code or learning a new program will be useful.

- Leverage family and friends to see if your student can assist them in any way. The key is to find a summer program that will add value and help the student get closer to knowing what he or she wants to do after college. Athletes may want to join a traveling club team or work with a coach to perfect their skills. If your student has no idea what he or she would like to study in college or do for a career, then I suggest a strong leadership camp. Also, keep in mind that this summer is the best time to test prep for the SAT/ACT. Have your student sign up early for a test prep class because the good ones will fill up fast.

Junior Year

- Sign up and take the PSAT.

- Your student will need to decide which test is the best option to achieve the highest score.

- Ask teachers for letter of recommendation.

- Does your student have all A's? Consider a tutor.

- Let their passion shine.

- Do all of the colleges who have contacted your student really want them to attend their school?

What to do Junior year:

October is a big month for high school juniors. Scoring well on the PSAT will open many doors for your student. There are over one million students who participate in the PSAT every October. Roughly the top 50% are notified that they are Commended Scholars. Commended Scholars receive a nice letter of recognition that students may add to their college applications. The top scoring 16,000 students are announced as National Merit Semi-Finalists. These semi-finalist students will get an opportunity to apply and continue in the competition for National Merit finalist. Many colleges offer scholarships to National Merit finalists.

The bottom line is that if your student becomes a National Merit finalist, he or she can earn a FREE college education!

- **Your student test prepped over the summer and took the PSAT in October, now what?** It is time to take the SAT/ACT. How does your student decide on which test to take and when to take the test? You will want to consider when the test prep is completed and the testing dates are available.

- **Your student will need to decide which test is the best option to score the highest.** If your student needs help deciding or wants a testing plan, it would be best to contact a college consultant.

- **Teachers are important (especially the good ones).** By this point, your student should have some favorite teachers. This will be very important when students choose which teachers they will ask to write their letters of recommendation. Before your student leaves for summer break it is a good idea to ask 3 teachers to write their college application letter of recommendation. Be mindful which teachers know your student best and which ones will take the time to write a great letter of recommendation. Your student will never see the letter that is written. It will go directly to the college.

- **Does your student have all A's?** If not, then you may need to consider getting a tutor. The honor societies at your student's high school offer tutoring for free as part of their community service. If your student is too busy before or after school, you may want to consider hiring a professional tutor. Finding a great tutor could be exactly what your student needs to get an A in a tough subject. Keep in mind that the core subjects will be on the ACT/SAT test, and your student will most likely take the subject again in college.

- **Your student's junior year is the time to let their passion shine**. If your student is *not* having fun, then he or she is missing out on doing things he or she enjoys. Writing a college application without passion will be a waste of time for the writer and the reader. The essay is used to add the final piece to the application puzzle. Colleges want to know who students are and what they're passionate about. There are only so many hours in the day to be productive; it is best that the time be used on something your student loves to do.

- **Do all of the colleges who have contacted your student really want them to attend their school**? Has your son or daughter been receiving mail and emails from potential colleges? This can be an exciting time for your family and it may be hard to decipher what is real and what is not.

I will share a little secret with you – taking the PSAT/SAT/ACT triggered most, but not all the mail your student is receiving. Colleges send out blanket "we want you" letters to try to boost their numbers. The more applicants that apply to a college make them look good. The low acceptance rate is not *reality* because most students that apply due to this mail blast should not be applying to that college. Now the application numbers go up and the acceptances go down. The college now looks very desirable and exclusive. Be careful and only apply to colleges that make sense for your student.

Senior Year

- Put it all together.

- Pick colleges to apply to.

- Should your student attend college visits at their high school?

- Write essays.

- Complete applications.

- Send transcripts.

- Send test scores.

- Getting organized.

- Celebrate all the accomplishments your student has achieved.

What to do Senior year:

Well, you have made it! The fun is just beginning, and all your hard work will pay off very soon. Just stay focused on the application deadlines, and keep your student motivated to complete applications.

- Now the big question comes to mind: how will you pay for college? If you have been planning academically and financially for the last four years, you should be well prepared. If you are picking up this book for the first time and your student is a senior, you may be freaking out!

- **Paying for college is now the #1 public fear of all Americans. Unfortunately, what you do not know will cost you.** Read everything you can, ask knowledgeable professionals a lot of questions, and hire a professional college consultant if you are not sure how you will pay for college. There are many myths about college funding, and buyer beware: you do not need to pay full price. Since I have covered this information in another chapter, I will summarize what you will want to do during this year.

Consider your options:

- Can you pay for college from your savings account without going into debt?

- Have you saved some money for college, and do you need to look at other options to fill in the financial gap?

- Are you going to make your student pay for his or her own college?

- Have you filled out the FAFSA?

- Do you know what your expected family contribution is going to be?

- Will your student receive a Merit scholarship?

- Will your student receive grants or scholarships?

- Has your student applied for local scholarships? The best scholarships often come from the parent's work or unions.

- Have you filled out the necessary paperwork to receive money from the colleges your student maybe attending? The majority of free money will come from your student's college.

- **Communication is very important in the college application process**. I suggest having an email address that is solely for the college application process. Set up an email account that is not spam-guarded, that your student will check daily, and is appropriate for college admissions. A good email address is firstnamelastname@gmail.com.

- **Should your student attend college visits at their high school**? Yes, if your student is considering that college, the more information they receive, the better. It is also another opportunity to ask questions and show interest in that school. If there is a sign-in sheet, make sure your student signs in.

- **The time has come to pick colleges to which your student will apply.** If you have no idea where to start, refer to my chapter on picking the right school. If you still have no idea where to apply, then ask your high school counselor for advice. Or, hire a professional college consultant who can pick the best colleges suited for your student.

- **Getting organized is going to be very helpful for the application season.** I give every student a three-ring binder with dividers to help them stay organized.

- **It is now time to apply to colleges.** The different applications open on different dates. Your student will want to write down all the important dates to remember. Deadlines are just that; nothing will be accepted after the college deadlines have passed.

- **Should my student apply for early decision?** Early decision admission programs allow your student to apply early, and if he or she gets in and loves it, no other applications are needed. We like to call this *one and done!* By applying for early decision, you are telling the college that if you are accepted, you are 100% committed to going there. When you get accepted to an early decision college, your student will be forced to withdraw applications from all other colleges. The downside is that your student will not have many financial options.

- **If you are hoping for some kind of financial aid, your student will want to apply for early action or regular decision.** Procrastination will be a huge problem for your student in this process. If students miss a deadline, they will not be able to apply to that college until the following year. Unlike early decision, early action allows your student to apply early to show their interest in a college, but it is not binding if they get accepted. The biggest benefit of applying for early action is that it reduces the stress of having to wait for a decision. Early decision deadlines are in November, and regular decision deadlines are from December through January.

- **What are secondary supplements, and does my student have to complete them?** In addition to the Common application, many colleges will also require their own supplement. This can be completed on the Common application site if the college participates in the Common application, but it will have to be done on the college's individual website if not.

- **Aren't all essays the same**? The answer is no; college application essays are very different for high school English class essays. Since a high school English teacher has not been taught how a college essay reader views an essay, it would be a bad idea to have your student's high school English teacher proofread the college application essay. They are looking for something totally different. It is always best to have a professional application editor proof your student's essays before they are submitted. Not all essays are created equal, and the essay could be the deal breaker.

- **College application fees and what you should expect**. Although applying to college usually is not as expensive as actually attending college, there are a number of associated fees. Most range from $40-$90, and can be paid in a number of ways (or waived).

  o If a college uses a Common Application, the fee can be paid through the Common Application website with a credit card.

  o If a college does not use the Common Application, they will provide instructions on how to pay the fee.

  o Fee waivers are available if your student qualifies. You will want to check with each school for details. Fees are typically due upon submission of the application.

- For students who are applying to a specialized program such as art, architecture, music, dance or theater, they may be asked to submit a portfolio of work. Make sure to check with your student's college; each has different requirements. There is also an additional information section in the Common Application where students can upload any extra information they wish to share with colleges.

- If your student makes any changes to his or her spring class schedule, your student will have to report the changes to all of the colleges that were applied to.

- Community service hours should be logged in and submitted to your student's high school. This is a great time to finish the service project or transfer it to a younger student.

- For students who wish to update applications after the original deadline, many guidance counselors may be willing to send a mid-semester update some time during the spring semester. This may include any awards that your student has won, accommodations given or generally anything that might bolster an application. Remember: this is just an update, so you will have had to submit the full application by the original due date first.

- A college may request additional testing. SAT Subject Tests may be requested to demonstrate mastery in a specific area.

- What is TOEFL, and does my student need to worry about it? If your student is from a non-English speaking country or is a non-native English speaker, he or she may be required to take the TOEFL to show proficiency in English. Check with your student's colleges to see if this is required.

- I always suggest starting with the end result in mind. What do I mean? Help your student think about what they would like to do after they graduate college.

- Do they want to have a career in social services, law enforcement, medical, engineering, or education, etc.? What is your student's potential income going to be once they graduate college? Does it make sense to go into debt for the career they want, or would they be better of going to a less expensive college? Would it be best for your student to be at a college where they graduate the top of their college class?

- These are all things to consider *before* applying to college. Have a plan that makes sense for your student and your family. If your student has hopes of going on to grad school, where will the money come from? Will an undergrad education set your student up for grad school acceptance? Every decision must be planned out so the student will spend the least amount of time in college and save money by knowing where is the best place to invest.

- After the college acceptances arrives, what happens? Your student still needs to finish strong. Some colleges will check final grades, and they can rescind their offer. Senioritis is real, and many students struggle to stay focused after spring break. Remember: they still have AP testing, Subject testing, and finals to accomplish. AP exams matter, and if a student took an AP class, he or she should sign up and take the AP exam. If your student gets a 3 or better on the AP test, he or she may not have to take the same class in college. This will save both time and money! Every college has their own guidelines when it comes to the AP score so you will want to check the college's policy. If you research this information before applying to college you may be able to pick a college where your student will be able to start as a sophomore. In other words, you can save a year of tuition. This is a huge savings!

- Planning your next move will be important emotionally to your student and financially to your family. Discussing all your options with your student can be stressful but very important. I put together a spreadsheet for my students to show them their options. Which colleges offer the best financial package, graduate in four years, is the best deal for the money, and have a success rate with job placement.

Making the Final College Decision

1. Focus on YOU - what is the best fit for you.

2. Focus on the reality of the school – does it match you.

3. Is it a good fit socially.

4. Review the curriculum – dig into your major.

5. Is it a fit financially.

- After your student has said YES to accept a college offer, what happens next? Here are some last-minute details that will need to be done:
  - o Most colleges now give the student a special website with their own mailbox. I suggest this email be activated ASAP and checked at least once a day. All communication will come through this email including scholarships and grants. You do not want to miss any deadlines for awards. This information is time sensitive.
  - o Check with your student's high school counselor regarding what his or her school does regarding Cal Grants. Most colleges do the work, but not all. The Cal Grant commission must verify your student's GPA. Most schools do this electronically. Cal Grants are need-based scholarships going up to $12,000 for UC colleges. If your student participates in a Home School Program, the system is a bit different. Colleges will want to see their SAT/ACT scores. If you need help with this, please ask a professional.
  - o Accept the financial aid offer or make an appointment to appeal it.

- o Send your student's final transcript to their college.
- o Complete housing and health forms.
- o Start searching for that perfect roommate. Be brutally honest when answering the roommate questionnaire.
- o Submit AP scores.
- o Register for the Orientation program at the college your student will be attending.
- o Hug your family and friends, and send out thank you cards to all the supporters who helped get through the process.

CONGRATULATIONS, YOU DID IT!

Parents – take some time to reflect on all that your student has accomplished, and celebrate with them to show your support. There are still many details that need to be completed, but you now have time to relax and enjoy. For students, it is now time to celebrate graduation from high school and dream of future plans. Wear college letters with pride, and remember how hard you worked to get what you wanted.

CHAPTER 8

Finances: College Without Student Loans – Fact Or Fiction

Is it possible to attend college and graduate without a student loan? Yes. I have helped many students navigate the financial process. With a strategic plan, it is possible. Below are two students who have recently graduated from college and their financial success story.

COLLEGE READY CASE STUDY: FINANCES

Kathy came to me as a freshman; she had big dreams but little money. I helped her formulate a plan to leverage the PSAT as well as a strategy to increase her GPA. After four years of working together, Kathy was accepted into 11 colleges and chose Harvard. Harvard met 100% of Kathy's financial need. Working hard and having a plan, made Kathy's dream of going to Harvard a reality!

Susan came to me as a junior with a dream of becoming a professional photographer. Her desire was to attend Chapman University in California. Financially speaking, her parents could afford Chapman but Susan did not want to burden her parents. With that in mind, we worked together to create a portfolio that would win her a full scholarship to Chapman. Susan's parents could not be happier with the result. They used some of Susan's college savings and took a nice long vacation after Susan left for college. They also bought a new car with the money saved in just the first year. (Their savings were not part of a 529 plan.)

I share these student success stories to share the reality of what great planning can do for a student. There are many more client stories just like these happy endings to a long journey. Planning is the key to not having to take out a student loan.

What you do not know will cost you!

Here Are the Common Mistakes Families Make When Saving For College:

- **WAITING TOO LONG TO START TO SAVE** –Some families consider college costs when it is already too late. The best time to start planning for college is when your children are toddlers.

- **PUTTING MONEY IN THE WRONG SAVINGS ACCOUNTS** – Not all savings accounts will protect your money from the government for college. Working with a college financial planner is the best way to learn where your money is safe. That said, for college financial planning, I recommend hiring a professional.

- An analogy I like to use is doing your taxes. You have two choices when it comes to doing them: 1) You could do your taxes and pay what the bottom line says, or 2) You could hire an accountant to advise you on the best strategy to take to help you pay the least amount of money to IRS.

- The same is true when it comes to paying for college: You can choose where you want to save your money and maybe get a 1-2% return, or you could hire a financial advisor who specializes in college financial planning. A specialist like this would advise you that there are many options for you. Knowing your options and having time to implement the best strategy is how you send your student to college without a student loan.

- **NO SAVING PLAN** – You will face the reality of college when your student gets there. This strategy could actually benefit you if you are a "need based" family. If you have nothing to offer colleges, and your student is a strong academic student, colleges may meet 100% of their need. This becomes a huge problem, however, if your student is an average student.

- Colleges do not pay for average students; therefore, your student may not receive any money from the college and will have to depend on government aid.

- **WE DON'T NEED TO SAVE...WE HAVE PLENTY OF MONEY TO PAY FOR COLLEGE** – You might have the funds today, however, it's smart to have a backup plan just in case your financial situation changes. If you have extra money to invest at the end of the year, there are safe places to secure your money for your student. There are also really bad places to save your money that will hurt your student's chances of getting scholarships and grants. Working with a professional who knows all the unique strategies that are safe for you and your student is very important for the future.

- **NOT TAKING THE PSAT THEIR JUNIOR YEAR** – If your student chooses not to take this test, they are choosing not to get a free or reduced education.

- **NOT TAKING THE AP EXAMS** – If your student chooses not to take the AP exams, they are choosing to give up the chance for a free year of college. **Yes, a free year of college at many colleges!** If your student takes enough AP exams and scores a 3 or better on the AP exams, there are many colleges that will let your student enter as a sophomore. This means you will save one year of college tuition.

- **NOT TAKING ANY COLLEGE OR DUAL-ENROLLMENT ENROLLMENT CLASSES WHILE IN HIGH SCHOOL** – If your student chooses *not* to take the most challenging

121

classes available to them, they are choosing to give up potential money from colleges. Some of my students take online college classes while they are in high school or during the summer months. This gives them a huge advantage if they get good grades in these classes.

Colleges like to see rigor. If your student demonstrates that he or she can handle the tough classes, colleges will want them. If colleges want them, they will be offered money!

Unfortunately, there are so many ways to make mistakes financially, and most of the time; it is because families simply do not know any better. As mentioned earlier, you have options. Hiring a professional who can help explain your options will save you both time and money.

Understanding financial aid and student loans is not easy for the average person. There is a lot of small print, and the buyer must beware. Do not sign anything without thoroughly understanding the terms and conditions. Please do not assume anything when it comes to college finances. Always be sure to ask a lot of questions.

ARE YOU FINANCIALLY COLLEGE READY?

Take this short quiz and see how you score! This will not be graded or used against you in the college process.

1. **Since our family has not been able to save anything for college, my student's only option is community college. True or <u>False</u>?**

   – Families who have not been able to save will likely find that their expected family contribution will be very low.

   – Parent contribution can be paid from savings, current income, or loans.

   o It is not expected all at once but over the course of a year.

   o Tuition payment plans are also available.

- Another option is to fill out the FAFSA before your student's senior year (be aware of deadlines). You will also want to see what your EFC or expected family contribution is going to be.

2. **Only rich students go to elite expensive colleges. True or <u>False</u>?**

- The higher the cost of college, the easier it is to demonstrate financial need.

- Many elite colleges offer to pay 100% of what your family can't pay.

- Studies have shown that the parental incomes of students in private colleges are, on average, lower than incomes of student's at large state universities.

- If your student has good grades, elite colleges want them and will pay for them!

3. **Only students from really low-income families qualify for financial aid. True or <u>False</u>?**

- Most financial aid is reserved for needy families. However, there are many forms of assistance to help families meet their expected contribution, like low-interest loans, grants, and scholarships.

4. **Only students with the best grades qualify for financial aid. True or <u>False</u>?**

- Some scholarships are "merit-based;" They are awarded based on the student's academic performance.

- Most financial aid is "need-based;" It is awarded based on the family's ability to pay for college.

5. **I need to pay a service to find scholarships for college. True or <u>False</u>?**

- Most financial aid and scholarship applications are free.

- There are no guarantees that you will win a scholarship.

- The information is available for free. If it is too good to be true, it might be a scam!

- The best scholarships are found at your student's college-to-be.

6. **The costs of a college education just are not worth it. True or <u>False</u>?**

- A college education will give your student more job opportunities, greater knowledge, wider perspective, and the chance to mature.

- Statistically, a student with a 4-year college degree will earn a million dollars more in his or her lifetime than a high school graduate.

7. **A college can cost as much as $75,000 a year. True or <u>False</u>?**

- There are some private colleges where tuition costs more than a new car.

- Most students attend colleges where tuition is much lower.

- The average tuition and fees for a 4-year public college is $9,655 in state.

8. **I am going to be the only student on financial aid and everyone will know. True or <u>False</u>?**

- 60% of all full-time students receive some kind of financial aid at a 4-year college.

- At some private colleges, 75% of the students receive some form of financial aid.

- Your student will find that receiving some type of aid is the norm, not the exception.

9. **All debt is bad debt. Student loans are always bad. True or <u>False</u>?**

- Actually, student loans are good debt. With a college degree, you are increasing your earning potential.

- If planned properly, the loan repayments are manageable. Consider that loan payback may not be painful if your student graduates college with a great job.

10. **If my kid is a star athlete, they will get a full ride scholarship and grades are secondary. True or <u>False</u>?**

   - On average, only 1% of graduates receive athletic scholarships.

   - Most college scholarships are given to sports that generate the most money.

   - Many colleges split scholarships among the new recruits so everyone feels like they are getting something.

   - For specific information on college athletes, go to www.ncaa.org.

Applying to multiple colleges is a good financial strategy. Make sure that you have applied to some colleges in which your student will be at the top of his or her class. Beginning in March (some colleges will be sooner), your student will receive multiple acceptance and award letters. Doing a comparison and analysis of the award letters will help put the financial picture into perspective.

What do award letters include?

SAMPLE UNIVERSITY

Dear Joe Sample:

GENERAL INFORMATION
The Office of University Financial Aid has prepared this statement using the following criteria:

Academic Level: Undergraduate Freshman
Dependency Status: Dependent
College: Undergraduate
Major/Program of Study: Non-Declared Major
Housing Category: On-Campus Housing

ESTIMATED COST OF ATTENDANCE:	$55,000
Tuition and fees:	$39,000
Housing and meals:	$13,000
Books and supplies:	$ 1,000
Personal and miscellaneous:	$ 2,000

AWARD

Description	Fall	Spring	Total	Accepted Y/N
President's Scholarship	$10,000.00	$10,000.00	$20,000.00	Y/N
Federal Pell Grant	$600.00	$600.00	$1,200.00	Y/N
Federal Supplemental Educational Opportunity Grant (FSEOG)	$500.00	$500.00	$1,000.00	Y/N
State Scholarship	$450.00	$450.00	$900.00	Y/N
Federal Work-Study (FWS)	$1,500.00	$1,500.00	$3,000.00	Y/N
Federal Perkins Loan	$1,250.00	$1,250.00	$2,500.00	Y/N
Federal Stafford Loan – Subsidized	$1,750.00	$1,750.00	$3,500.00	Y/N
Federal Stafford Loan – Unsubsidized	$1,000.00	$1,000.00	$2,000.00	Y/N
		Total:	$34,100.00	

If any of the information in the table above is incorrect, please contact the Office of Financial Aid in writing or via the Ask the Counselor service.

Office of University Financial Aid
Sample University, 199 State Street, 4th Floor, City, MA 02009
800.555.1212 www.sampleuniversity.edu

Financial award letters look different for all colleges. Below are the similarities you will want to compare:

- **Merit Aid/Scholarships:** Colleges award merit aid to deserving students using individual college guidelines. This aid is in the form of college-based grants and scholarships.

126

Some scholarships have criteria such as a specific GPA, enrollment requirement, or certain income requirements. Make sure to ask if the scholarship will be good for all four years, or whether your student will have to reapply every year. Scholarships help students pay for their own education; they do not have to be paid back. Scholarships are available to students who demonstrate achievement in academics, athletics, the arts, or community service. Scholarships may be awarded by the college or by other organizations.

- **Work Study:** If you qualify for financial aid, colleges will award you work study. This is money the student will earn at a job, usually on campus, while in college. This money can help to offset college expenses.

- **Federal and State Grants:** These awards do not need to be repaid. Some grants are based on a student's GPA.

- **Student Loans:** Colleges offer subsidized and unsubsidized student loans. A **subsidized loan** can be a good investment. The government pays the interest on the loan while the student is in college. They offer low interest rates, and multiple loans may be consolidated into a single payment. An **unsubsidized** loan has low interest rates; multiple loans can be consolidated into one payment. The recipient may opt to pay interest while enrolled, or you can allow interest to accumulate while enrolled and during the 6-month grace period.

- **Parent Loans:** Although some colleges add these to the award letter, these loans should *not* be considered part of the aid package. If they are included, subtract them from the overall total. With a parent "Plus" loan, parents can borrow up to the total cost of an education, minus any other aid the student receives. Plus loans have a variable interest rate. *Be very careful with these loans!*

Types of Federal Student Aid

GRANTS
(FREE money)
*usually based on financial need and
does not need to be repaid.

LOANS
(Borrowed money)
*must be repaid with interest

WORK STUDY
(Earned money)
*a job that lets you earn money
while you are in school

What is the best way to compare awards?

You can create a spreadsheet and compare each college. Comparisons to consider:

- Estimated Cost of Attendance
  - ✓ Tuition and fees
  - ✓ Housing and meals
  - ✓ Books and supplies
  - ✓ Transportation
  - ✓ Other costs?
- Grants and Scholarships your student will receive
  - ✓ Grants and scholarships from the college directly
  - ✓ Federal Pell Grant
  - ✓ Grants from your state

- ✓ Other scholarships?
- • What Will You Be Responsible for Paying?
  - ✓ Cost of attendance minus total grants and scholarships
- • Options to consider
  - ✓ Work-study
  - ✓ Loan options
  - ✓ Family contributions
  - ✓ Payment plans offered by the college
  - ✓ Military benefits
  - ✓ Non-federal private education loan

How do you know which college is the best deal?

First, consider the colleges individually. Did they offer aid? Was the aid offered competitive, compared to the other colleges? Does this package make financial sense based on your student's desired career?

Second, compare each college side-by-side. Which college stands out as the best deal? If you are not happy with the financial package from one of your colleges, I recommend you appeal it using your other college offers as leverage.

Determining what is the best college for your student is not always easy. You will want to consider which college gave your student the most aid, excluding loans. This is what will allow your student to graduate with minimal debt in the least amount of time.

If you have exhausted all your options, here is what you will want to do to apply for financial aid: Complete the FAFSA (Free Application for Federal Student Aid). The FAFSA calculates your student's eligibility for need-based financial aid.

Changes to the FAFSA process for 2017–2018

YOU CAN SUBMIT THE FAFSA EARLIER

* Students will be able to file a 2017–18 FAFSA as early as October 1, 2016 rather than beginning on Jan. 1, 2017

YOU CAN USE EARLIER INCOME INFORMATION

Beginning with the 2017–18 /FAFSA, students will report income information from an earlier tax year.

Who should apply to the FAFSA? Every student who will be attending college should apply to the FAFSA. The most common response I get about FAFSA is, "Why should I apply for the FASFSA? I make too much money." What happens if your income changes tomorrow? Always have a plan B; it's like taking out college financial insurance. The second most popular question is, "What if I do not want to share my financial information?" The government already has your taxes. Your financial information is available to them. If you do not fill out the FAFSA, you are leaving potential money on the table.

If this all seems very confusing, you are not alone. You can either hire a professional to help you fill out your FAFSA, or you can pay someone to do it for you. If you would like to receive more information, below are some online resources:

- U.S. Department of Education – www.studentaid.ed.gov
- Electronic FAFSA – www.fafsa.ed.gov
- FastWeb – www.fastweb.com
- FinAid – www.finaid.org
- Collegiate Athletics – www.ncaa.org

CHAPTER 9

Free Money: Top Secrets To Getting Scholarships

There are 3 types of scholarships: Private, College-Given, and Athletic.

Private scholarships are often offered by a business, organization, or foundation; Private scholarships can be merit-based, need based, or both.

The colleges themselves give college scholarships. The college-awarded athletic scholarships have become very difficult to get. If you have a scholar athlete, I suggest you memorize the NCAA rules and follow them 100%.

Who does not dream of sending their student to college for free? Everyone I work with would like to receive free money that they do not have to pay back. If finding a legitimate scholarship is not difficult enough, winning one is almost impossible.

BELOW ARE 10 SECRETS TO HELP YOU FIND AND WIN SCHOLARSHIPS:

Secret #1 – The reality is that most full ride scholarships come from the college in a merit or athletic award.

Once your student has applied to a college and has been accepted, start looking through that school's website for scholarship opportunities. Another option is to contact the college's financial aid office, and ask about how to find their scholarship applications and deadlines. Not every school will offer your student a scholarship, but it is worth asking.

Secret #2 – Private scholarships are available to everyone!

Here are the biggest and most well-known:

- **Gates Millennium Scholars Program** - The Gates Millennium Scholars (GMS) program, established in 1999, is a 1.6-billion-dollar initiative funded by grant from the Bill & Melinda Gates Foundation. The goal of the GMS program is to "promote academic excellence and to provide an opportunity for outstanding minority students with significant financial need to reach their highest potential." (This information is taken directly from the GMS website).

- **Stamps Scholarship Program**– The Stamps Foundation, with its partner schools, seeks students who demonstrate academic merit, strong leadership potential, and exceptional character. As the Stamps Foundation web site notes, "We support exceptional young people with promise and vision who are eager to make their contribution to the world and have the work ethic to make their dreams a reality. Leadership development is at the core of the Stamps Scholarship program. Leadership potential is also a key part of the selection criteria for receiving a Stamps award. The Stamps Foundation welcomes and supports students from all backgrounds and areas of study. Financial need is not a consideration. At some of our partner schools, international students are eligible for the Stamps Scholarship. Students should check directly with the program that they are interested in to view eligibility requirements."

- **QuestBridge College Match Scholarships** – As the Questbridge web site states, "The QuestBridge National College Match is a college and scholarship application process that helps outstanding low-income high school seniors gain admission and *full four-year scholarships* to the nation's most selective colleges".

- **Chick Evans Caddie Scholarship** –For students who have worked as caddies, there are great opportunities. According to the web site for the Chick Evans Caddie Scholarship, "The Chick Evans Caddie Scholarship is a full tuition and housing college scholarship for golf caddies that is renewable for up to four years. Each year, more than 900 deserving caddies across the country attend college on a four-year scholarship from the Evans Scholars Foundation. Selected applicants must have a strong caddie record, excellent grades, outstanding character and demonstrated financial need."

- **Coca Cola Scholars Program** – As noted on the Coca Cola Scholars Program web site, "The Coca-Cola Scholars Program Scholarship is an achievement-based scholarship awarded to graduating high school seniors. Students are recognized for their capacity to lead and serve, as well as their commitment to making a significant impact on their schools and communities. With the 28th class in 2016, the Foundation has provided over 5,700 Coca-Cola Scholars with more than $60 million in educational support. 150 Coca-Cola Scholars are selected each year to receive this $20,000 scholarship."

- **Horatio Alger Scholarship Programs** – As the Horatio Alger scholarship web site explains, "The Horatio Alger Association honors the achievements of outstanding individuals in our society who have succeeded in spite of adversity and who are committed to supporting young people in pursuit of increased opportunities through higher education."

- **Jack Kent Cook Foundation College Scholarship Programs** – According to the Jack Kent Cook Foundation web site: "This scholarship rewards excellence by supporting high-achieving high school seniors with financial need who seek to attend the nation's best four-year colleges and universities."

- **AXA Achievement Scholarship** – As the AXA Achievement scholarship site states, "The AXA Achievement Scholarship provides over $1.4 million in scholarships to young people throughout the nation representing all 50 states, Washington DC and Puerto Rico. Students have the opportunity to receive a $2,500, $10,000 or $25,000 scholarship. In addition, for every student who wins a scholarship, a grant in the amount of $1,000 will be made to the winner's school."

- **Buick Achievers**– According to the Buick Achievers web site, "In just five years, the Buick Achievers Scholarship program has provided students with more than $30 million in scholarships to help them achieve their dreams."

- **Marshall Scholarships** – As noted on the Marshall scholarships web site, "Marshall Scholarships finance young Americans of high ability to study for a graduate degree in the United Kingdom. Up to forty Scholars are selected each year to study at graduate level at an UK institution in any field of study. As future leaders, with a lasting understanding of British society, Marshall Scholars strengthen the enduring relationship between the British and American peoples, their governments and their institutions. Marshall Scholars are talented, independent and wide-ranging, and their time as Scholars enhances their intellectual and personal growth. Their direct engagement with Britain through its best academic programs contributes to their ultimate personal success."

- **Rhodes Scholarships** – The Rhodes web site notes that: "The Rhodes Scholarships are the oldest and most celebrated international fellowship awards in the world. Each year 32 young students from the United States are selected as Rhodes Scholars, through a decentralized process representing the 50 states, the District of Columbia, and the U.S. territories. Applicants from more than 320

American colleges and universities have been selected as Rhodes Scholars."

- **Winston Churchill Scholarship** – According to its web site, "The Churchill Scholarship provides funding to American students for a year of Master's study in science, mathematics, and engineering at the University of Cambridge."

- **Harry S. Truman Scholarship** – The information on the Harry S. Truman web site states that: "The Truman is a very competitive national scholarship. Each year, the Foundation reviews over 600 applications for our 55 to 65 Scholarships awarded annually."

- **Henry Luce Foundation Scholarship** – According to the Henry Luce web page: "The Luce Scholars Program is a nationally competitive fellowship program. It was launched by the Henry Luce Foundation in 1974 to enhance the understanding of Asia among potential leaders in American society. The program provides stipends, language training, and individualized professional placement in Asia for 15-18 Luce Scholars each year, and welcomes applications from college seniors, graduate students, and young professionals in a variety of fields who have had limited exposure to Asia."

Secret #3 – There are legitimate websites to help with your scholarship search.

I have had students win scholarships from the list below. There are many others, but be careful and research them thoroughly. Be careful not to give out too much personal information. The more information you give, the more advertising you will receive!

GOOD SCHOLARSHIP WEB SITES

- www.fastweb.com
- www.cappex.com
- www.scholarships.com

- www.zinch.com
- www.chegg.com
- www.collegedata.com
- www.kaarme.com
- www.collegeprowler.com

Secret #4 – Look for scholarships from your employer, unions, department stores, or even your high school's PTA or PTC. There are some crazy ways to get awards.

There was one last year through my daughter's high school PTA that she won because she was a Cheerleader all 4 years and in Leadership all 4 years. These scholarships are usually smaller, but they are quick and easy to apply to. The competition is smaller, and your chances of winning an award are greater. You may find these scholarships through your student's high school counseling office, local organizations like the Elks, Rotary Club, Lions Club, Knights of Columbus, local women's clubs, Masons, Optimists, Kiwanis, Jaycees, newspapers, or online.

Secret #5 – There are no tricks, but there *is* just good old hard work and follow through.

Deadlines are critical. Directly and thoroughly answering the prompt for the essay is very important. Help your student realize that the scholarship application readers want to get to know them. They consider: What are your student's passions? What have these students accomplished? Why should one receive the award over another student?

What will *increase your student's* chances of winning? High GPA, test scores, class rank, community service hours and leadership. Also, a strong essay will usually get the scholarship. I encourage all of my students to take their time and to get the essay edited by a professional.

Secret #6 – Passion = Scholarships!

Seek scholarships that your student has shown passion in like, art, dance, theater, mock trial, leadership, community service, etc. It is important to highlight your student's unique talents or accomplishments.

Secret #7 – Consider your background.

Many scholarships give money to students with particular ethnic or racial backgrounds. There are even scholarships for students in military families, students with parents in volunteer organizations and Greek societies. There are also a lot of scholarships designed for students who are returning to school late in life.

Secret #8 – If a scholarship advertises "no essay," do not waste your student's time applying.

I have found that this is just a way to fish for your personal information and then sell it to other college lists like loan companies, etc.

Secret #9 – If your student does not go looking for a scholarship, it will not come to them.

The chances of your student getting a private scholarship without researching and applying are 0%. On the flip side of that, your student could spend hundreds of hours researching and applying to private scholarships and get zero awards. There is no guarantee; it is a competition, and only the best application wins. Please *do* keep in mind if your student is chasing these private scholarships and their grades drop, they may lose their chance to go to college.

Secret #10 – Have your student follow directions carefully.

Answer each and every question. Do not assume the scholarship organization knows anything about your student. If there is a word count on the essay, adhere to it. If samples of your work are required, give them the best you have. Have someone double check and proofread everything in the application. Build a spreadsheet to keep track of your deadlines!

Preparing your application for scholarships – what you should know:

- Keep all your backup data in one place and only send copies. It will be prudent to maintain a master file of all academic records, transcripts from every high school and college your student has attended, SAT/ACT/Subject test scores; tax information, any financial aid forms, and other details about you like your passport or birth certificate. Do not wait until these documents are asked for. I suggest having copies ready to send well in advance so your student will not miss any deadlines.

- Put together a resume of all extracurricular activities. This can include, but not limited to: how your student spent his or her time while not in school, sports, community service, work etc.

- Print out, and practice filling out the scholarship applications before you send out the final copy.

- Type your application directly into the form if you have access to a computer, or use your best writing without erasing or mistakes.

- Make sure to include enough postage if sending in snail mail. A certified mail/delivery receipt is always a good idea.

I often get asked, "How many scholarships should a student apply for?" My answer is, "As many as they have time for."

It is a numbers game, and luck can also be a factor. Find scholarships that fit your student's unique passions or talents. If your student has the time after studying for their classes, testing, community service, leadership, band, sport etc. then they should be applying for scholarships. If your student is barely holding all A's or has not received the test scores necessary for college, then spending time chasing private scholarships, does not make much sense.

A few last thoughts on private scholarships:

1. Stay organized

2. Record the deadlines, and note the manner in which you submitted the application.

3. Start early on the essay so your student will have time to get it edited.

4. Send in all necessary documentation like – transcript, teacher recommendation letters, test scores etc.

5. Have your student write a thank you letter once he or she receives any award.

College given scholarships or as some call it the 'Automatic Merit Scholarship' and how can your student get one:

First, you may be wondering what is an automatic merit scholarship? This type of scholarship is the best to receive! Why? Because it happens without you or your student having to do anything. The colleges have parameters regarding specific criteria like GPA or test scores to name only a few. This type of scholarship is used to get students to enroll at their college. These scholarships can be full tuition or a full ride (includes everything). Each college has different parameters, and a good College Consultant can lead you to the colleges that offer the most Automatic Merit Scholarships.

Second, how do you find this type of scholarship? You could look on each and every college website and see if you could find them. However, be aware this will take a lot of time and patience. Or, you could hire a College Planning professional who could help you find all the Merit Scholarships offered by colleges around the country. What you do not know will cost you both time and money.

The Athletic Scholarship – who actually gets a full ride?

According to the NCAA website, only about 2% of high school athletes are awarded athletic scholarships to compete in college. Very few of the 2% become professional athletes. If you have a scholar athlete, it is very important to follow the exact rules of the NCAA. There are two divisions that offer money to athletes.

Division 1 and some Division 2 schools give more than two billion dollars in athletic scholarships each year to more than 150,000 student-athletes. Division 3 schools do *not* offer athletic scholarships. If your student is talented enough to get offered a full scholarship, it will cover tuition and fees, room, board and course-related books.

Most student-athletes receive only a partial scholarship so that more students can be given some kind of award. Keep in mind: many schools will only offer one year at a time, and the scholarship will have to be renewed yearly. If the student is playing well and keeping grades up, then he or she will have nothing to worry about.

A WORD OF CAUTION AS YOUR STUDENT APPLIES TO SCHOLARSHIPS

Do not overlook what is so easy to find. What does your student look like if a scholarship were to Google your student's name? Make sure to remove any inappropriate social media or Internet material, and create a professional email address.

CHAPTER 10

College Admissions: Interviews And The Waiting Game

The excitement is building. Every day your student is checking his or her email looking for that perfect college acceptance letter. Tears of happiness and maybe a few frustrated moments are sure to find their way into your home. Each day, your student is waiting to hear back from first-choice colleges. What can your student do during this exciting-yet-frustrating time of waiting?

I recommend using this time to go on admissions interviews, to plan Spring Break college tours, to continue to focus on GPA, and to apply for scholarships.

There are colleges that will not make their decision on your student's acceptance, until they have been interviewed by an admissions advisor or alumni (if you are out of state). Your student will want to use this interview to his or her advantage. This is the last time students will have the opportunity to shine. This interview will offer your student an opportunity for an exchange of information. The interview represents a chance to ask well thought-out questions and a chance to highlight student strengths and interest in the college.

Before the interview:

- Help your student prepare by practicing interviewing with another adult.

- Research the college website for information that you find interesting or impressive. These are good talking points!

- Write them down on a notepad, and bring them up during the interview.

- It is also a good idea to have your student bring a copy of their most recent transcript and resume.

Some interviews will be done over the computer, and I suggest that families take time to make sure that everything – including the microphone – works great on your computer; you do not want to be surprised by technological snafus.

Take the time to be mindful of what your student will wear for a campus interview. It should be clean and conservative, such as professional attire. If you can't afford slacks and a tie or a dress, it would be best to borrow something appropriate.

Before greeting the in-person interviewer, have your student practice with a firm and confident handshake. Have them practice shaking hands while looking a stranger in the eye. I know this may sound elementary, but most students have never been in this formal interview situation before. The basics are very important.

The interviewer is looking for anything that does not match your student's application or essay. Colleges are looking to see if the student has confidence and social skills to be successful in college. Practice, practice and practice some more. I spend a whole day working on interview skills with my student's, it is very important.

Remember, the interview is like an icing on a cake. It can make the cake look pretty and finished, or it can melt and fall apart. Also, do not forget to send a personalized, handwritten thank you note to the interviewer; it will go a long way.

Spring Break is a great time to visit/tour your student's top 3 colleges. Not only is it a great family-bonding trip, but it is also a time for your student to have a reality check. As the school year comes to a close, the reality of leaving for college becomes real. Some students embrace it and start to plan for what they will bring to college and when they leave for school. Other students become very quiet and distant. They maybe have a difficult time imagining that they will not see their family members daily. Some students become terrified and start to second-guess going to college at all. One of my students asked me who would make them food and do their laundry? Most students are a little fearful of the unknown.

By going to the potential colleges with your student, you can address all of their concerns so that your student can make the best decision for him or herself. Some students cannot wait to live in a new state, while others are very content to continue to live at home. Most colleges will have sent out their acceptances by Spring Break, but not all of them. Try not to jump to conclusions or make assumptions. Some colleges just take longer than others.

College tours: What is important to look for at this point in the decision process?

If your student has only taken a virtual tour of their top schools because they were too far away or because it is cost prohibitive for them, this tour will be critical. If you have been on all the campuses before, then you will want to look for certain things about the campus that may concern you, such as safety.

11 SUGGESTIONS THAT WILL HELP YOU MAKE THE MOST OF YOUR COLLEGE VISIT:

1. **Act like you are on vacation:** Combine college visits with adventure. Your student will love it! If you're in California, try something like stopping at Pismo Beach and riding quads on the sand. It is a great way to clear your head if you are visiting more than one college a day. Go to a museum or a local sports event. Try something you or your student has never done or seen.

2. **Work as a team:** Plan and prepare for your trip together. If your student has a driver's license and you are taking a

road trip, have him or her share in the driving. Alternatively, have your student be your navigator.

3. **Stay in the moment:** Try your best to leave work at home. Limit the amount of time you or your student is on the phone. Keep the conversation light, and focus on the adventure.

4. **Once you get to the college: Start at the Admissions office.**

   a. At this point in the process, I recommend going on the guided tour. You will need to sign up ahead of time either online or by a phone appointment.

   b. Do not rush this time on campus. If there is a social event or play, attend it. Spend some time looking at the dorms. Consider questions for future planning: Will your student have an option to pick which dorm they want to live in? How will roommates be selected? If you have not paid the housing security deposit, I suggest paying it ASAP. Some colleges have more students than they do housing, and it is important for a freshman to live on campus so they have easy access to the college.

   c. If religion is part of the college's required classes, look into attending a service.

5. **Your second stop should be the financial aid office. Here are some questions you might want to ask:**

   a. What is the total cost of college or financial aid budgeted cost?

   b. What forms are used by the college to determine financial aid eligibility (FAFSA, CSS Profile etc.)?

   c. What is the college's financial aid deadline? When will you know how much your student will be awarded?

   d. How does the college financially reward a good student?

e. What percentage of my financial NEED will be met by the college?

f. What percentage of this need met will be in the form of Gift Aid? In the forms of Loans? In the form of Work/Study?

g. What other non-need or merit grant and scholarships are available?

h. If any private outside scholarship is awarded, will the school use these to replace their own monies?

i. What is the average debt incurred by each student upon graduation?

6. **Have lunch in the student dining halls:** Try to have lunch when the student lunch area is busy. Sit in the middle of it, and take in the sounds and smells. This will give you a great feel for the student population. Later at dinner, ask your student about their thoughts regarding lunch. What did they like and dislike? Could you see your student living in that environment?

7. **Stay with a friend:** If you know anyone attending this school try to have a meal with them, or if possible, have your student stay the night.

8. **Class size and feel:** If possible, try to sit in on a class in session. This is a great way to show students the difference between high school and college. Pick a very large class with 330+ seats and pick a small class of 20 students or less. Your student will know right away which environment they prefer. If you get the opportunity to speak with a department head, here are some questions you may want to ask:

a. What is unique about this department's program?

b. What is the likelihood of graduating from this program in four years?

c. What department facilities and special technology are available?

d. How does the faculty advising system work?

e. How accessible are the professors in this department?

f. How many full-time professors are on the department staff?

g. What percentages of full-time professors teach introductory classes?

h. What is the average size of the classes or lectures?

9. **Find an interest in something other than academics:** Take a tour of Fraternity row or the Athletics department. Look into clubs or intramural sports. Attend a play or concert. Walk around the surrounding area and get a feel for the community. Focus on your student's passions and how he or she would find daily life at their new home.

10. **Spend time at the Career Placement Office:** Here are some questions you may want to ask.

a. How many full-time staff members work in the placement office?

b. What job placement services are provided by the placement office?

c. How long do job placement services remain in effect after graduation?

d. What percentage of graduates will be employed prior to graduation?

e. What are the most popular majors of graduates receiving employment?

f. Which companies and organizations recruit your graduates?

g. What are the credentials of those graduates receiving employment?

    h.   What is the starting salary of graduates in my field or major?

    i.   What is the future employment outlook of my field or major?

11. If your student is an Athlete, here are some questions you may want to ask the Athletic Department/Coach:

    a.   Where would your rank <your sport> at your college? In your league?

    b.   What sports or activities share the same facilities with <SPORT>?

    c.   Does the college plan any additions or changes to the facilities?

    d.   Does <SPORT> have an off-season schedule?

    e.   What locations are on the team's upcoming travel schedules?

    f.   What is the breakdown of the staff, coaches, and their specialties?

    g.   What allowances are made for class and exam preparation?

    h.   What are my earliest opportunities at playing my position?

    i.   Does the team have a set of rules or policies for the athletes?

NEXT, IT IS TIME FOR THE PROS AND CONS LIST.

On your trip home, compile a list of pros and cons for each college while it is still fresh in your mind. Have a discussion about why your student liked something or did not care for something at a particular college. This is the beginning of an exciting future. Remember to keep the conversation positive since this is a starting point. Compile a list of the colleges you would like to see next!

LAST, RANK YOUR COLLEGE CHOICES.

Based on the information you've gathered during your college visits. Now is the time to determine which colleges best fit your student's personality, meet the parents' priorities, and offer the family a good value.

Recognizing and fighting senioritis: how to help your student finish strong!

Senioritis: noun. A crippling disease that strikes high school seniors. Symptoms include: laziness, an excessive wearing of comfortable clothes, old athletic shirts, sweatpants, athletic shorts, and sweatshirts. Also, features a lack of studying, repeated absences, and a generally dismissive attitude. The only known cure is a phenomenon known as GRADUATION!

Did you know that colleges could rescind offers to students if their grades decline or if they are found doing inappropriate things on social media? It does not happen often, but there is a chance. I would never wish that problem on any student. Senioritis is real, and seems to get worse after Spring Break. It is always best to have an open discussion with your student on what can potentially happen if he or she makes poor choices. Every year, colleges rescind offers of admission, put students on academic probation, or alter financial aid packages as a result of some effects of "senioritis."

Colleges have the right to deny admission to an accepted applicant if the student's senior-year grades drop. Many letters of acceptance state this information directly on the letter of admission. Admission officials can ask a student to explain a drop in their grades and can revoke an offer of admission if they feel it is warranted. Colleges do not receive final grades until June or July, so students may not learn of a revoked admission until July or August, after they've given up spots at other colleges and have few options left.

COLLEGE READY CASE STUDY: SENIORITIS

I had a student who I will call Amber. Two years ago, she was accepted to Pepperdine, and she could not have been more excited to attend there the following fall. Amber had a 4.42 GPA and was a great student.

Unfortunately, Amber met some new friends on a spring break trip to the river that derailed her desire to work hard. These new friends convinced Amber to cut class and to hang out with them instead. Amber missed more classes in April than she had all four years in high school. Because of her absence, Amber's grades started to go down, and she got scared that she would lose her scholarship to Pepperdine.

What happened next, I will never forget. Amber made a poor decision to cheat on a history test. She was caught with the cheat sheet on the bottom of her shoe. Not only was Amber suspended from high school for three days, she lost her scholarship to Pepperdine. She could no longer afford to attend her dream school. Amber made a series of bad choices because she thought her future was secure. She got overly confident and believed that she was untouchable.

Please caution your student about what can be taken away and the ramifications of making poor choices—both during high school and throughout their college experience!

What colleges expect from your student:

- Colleges see both a midyear grade report and a final (year-end) transcript. They expect students to maintain previous levels of academic success. If your student always receives A's and B's, then a C or D may be a problem.

- Colleges expect seniors to complete courses that they are enrolled in, including high-level courses. If your student lists classes on a college application and then they decide to drop or change their classes, they must let the colleges they applied to know the new class schedule.

149

How to keep your Senior on track:

- Keep your student excited about going to college.

- Communicate openly about what can happen if they get lazy or lose focus.

- Have your student maintain a challenging course load. If they have always taken AP or Honors classes and they decide to take early release or basket weaving, they are sending the wrong message to colleges.

- Encourage your student to enjoy the last year of school. Suggest that they attend football games, go to the prom, attend graduation festivities, and participate in clubs, sports, and volunteer work.

- If your student needs something new and challenging, encourage them to commit to an internship or career-focused job. This will help them in the future to make sure they are majoring in a subject that they will love to call a career.

- Keep a calendar of your student's activities and deadlines. Help them to stay focused and prioritize what is most important. Focus on things like AP/Subject tests, college applications, senior-year events and extracurricular.

- Avoid constant nagging about applications and the application process. Try to keep a balance in your home of work and pleasure. All work and no play – and your senior will shut down.

Keeping your student focused in these ways will not only protect them against senioritis, but it will leave them in a stronger position to transition from high school to college.

Checklist For Success

(For those busy parents who do not have time to read the entire book)

- ✓ Create an individual plan for your student.
- ✓ Prepare a strategy with the end result in mind.
- ✓ Create a timeline that is specific and measurable.
- ✓ Have a plan A, but also have plans B and C!
- ✓ Determine your student's passions.
- ✓ Determine your student's talents and the qualities that make him or her stand out.
- ✓ Note your student's areas of opportunity.
- ✓ What will colleges remember about your student?
- ✓ Will your student play a sport or in college – do they have video footage to share?
- ✓ Will your student apply as an artist? Does your student have an up-to-date art portfolio?
- ✓ Should your student stay at his or her current high school or transfer to a better one?
- ✓ Has your student taken the most challenging classes available to him or her?
- ✓ Is the IB program worth transferring high schools for?
- ✓ Does your student's high school offer Dual enrollment?

✓ Is Dual enrollment a good choice for your student?

✓ Determine what GPA your student will need. Is it realistic?

✓ Ask for your student's class rank every semester. (Yes, it changes.)

✓ Determine what PSAT/SAT/ACT/AP/Subject test scores are needed. – Are they realistic?

✓ Which test should your student take – the SAT or ACT, or both?

✓ How will your student do test preparation?

✓ How many times will you have your student take the PSAT?

✓ Determine if your student is eligible for a test fee waiver.

✓ Will you student take the SAT Subject II tests?

✓ Understand how the National Merit Scholarship Program works.

✓ Determine how many AP/IB/Dual Enrollment/College classes your student will need to take. – Is this course load realistic?

✓ Is your student a strong test taker? Will he or she be an AP Scholar?

✓ Look for colleges with strong merit scholarships.

✓ Can your family afford college?

✓ Do not wait to start saving for college.

✓ Make sure you are putting your money in the best place for college.

✓ Discuss your financial strategy with a professional who is familiar with the FAFSA and EFC.

✓ Estimate your cost of attendance – tuition, housing, meals, books, supplies, transportation etc.

✓ Complete your EFC.

- ✓ Complete your FAFSA.

- ✓ Complete your CSS profile

- ✓ Determine which college is the best deal.

- ✓ If you need a loan, find out if you will qualify.

- ✓ Know your options: grants, scholarships, work study, and federal loans.

- ✓ Become familiar with interest rates.

- ✓ Look for colleges where your student will graduate in 4 years.

- ✓ Look for out-of-state public colleges or international schools with special pricing for out-of-state students.

- ✓ Look for private schools that meet 100% of need.

- ✓ If your student has taken AP classes, look for colleges who will honor the AP classes and allow your student to start as a Sophomore.

- ✓ Look for four-year commuter colleges that are close to home.

- ✓ Consider having your student take classes at a local community college during the summer and winter vacations.

- ✓ Assess your family finances ASAP.

- ✓ Decide whether your student's desired college is a want or a need.

- ✓ Determine what colleges will be the perfect match for your student.

- ✓ Pick a career to strive for.

- ✓ Pick a major. – Will it pay for their wants and needs after graduation?

- ✓ Consider the graduation rate at the colleges your student is considering.

✓ Review the acceptance rates at the colleges where your student is applying.

✓ What is your student looking for in a college?

✓ How will you decide which colleges to apply to?

✓ Do you know which colleges will be a reach, comfort, or safety college for your student?

✓ If your student got into the college, would they really want to live there?

✓ Will your student be happy at a religious college or at a school without religion?

✓ If your student gets accepted as a Scholar Athlete, will he or she get to live with non-athletes?

✓ If your student gets accepted as a Scholar Athlete, will he or she get to pick a major, or will the coach decide?

✓ If your student gets accepted as a Scholar Athlete, will he or she get playing time?

✓ If your student is a Merit Scholar, will he or she be happier being a big fish in a small school or a small fish in a big school?

✓ What is the reality of your student sticking with a chosen major?

✓ Have you visited enough colleges to know what your student wants?

✓ Have you toured a public college, private college, state college, religious college etc.?

✓ Consider the size of the college and how many large lectures they offer.

✓ Has your student selected a specific geographical region for schools?

✓ What is the total cost of each college your student is applying to ? (Consider the add-ons.)

✓ Determine the entire application process for each college your student is applying to.

✓ Document all deadlines, and check them often.

✓ Have your student contact 2-3 recommenders who would be willing to write a letter of recommendation to colleges.

✓ Create a resume highlighting everything your student has accomplished.

✓ Practice interviewing skills in person and via computer.

✓ Keep a list of all extracurricular activities your student has been involved in during high school.

✓ Have you logged all of your student's community hours? Note: Have they been signed off?

✓ Does your student's community service project tell the college something about your student?

✓ Can your student write an essay about his or her community service experience?

✓ Has your student lead other students who are older or younger than he or she is? Has your student lead others in a sport or band?

✓ Will your student's essay help the application reader get to know your student better?

✓ As much as you may think it is a good idea to write your students essay for them, don't do it.

✓ The essay is different from a high school English class essay. Pick the editor carefully.

✓ Compare award letters.

✓ Research which scholarships are available to your student.

✓ Apply for private scholarships.

✓ Apply for college given scholarships.

✓ Visit *at least* your final two colleges before you accept any college offer.

✓ Does your final college selection offer all the things that are important to you?

✓ Visit the career placement office.

✓ Complete a pros and cons list for your final school selections.

✓ Keep this book with you throughout the planning process.

✓ If this all seems too overwhelming, seek the help of your student's high school counselor or Internet resources. Contact colleges, and talk to other parents.

✓ View College Ready's website at:

www.collegereadyplan.com.

✓ Sign up for a free 30-minute consultation by going to:

http://collegereadyplan.com/free-call/

Thank you for reading!

I hope you enjoyed this book! I enjoyed putting it together because I know how much families struggle during this important time and I wanted to be of service.

CAN YOU DO ME A FAVOR PLEASE – It would help me spread the word to others, if you could write a review of it on Amazon. Having reviews helps people who are deciding whether to purchase the book make a decision. Reviews are not easy to get, so if you could take a few minutes to write one, I would be greatly obliged.

Go to Amazon now to write a review:

https://www.amazon.com/dp/B06Y5CNSYD

Remember, to pick up your FREE Gift, *15 Ways to Get a Reduced or FREE College Tuition* at:

http://collegereadyplan.com/sign-up/

Glossary

ACT (American College Testing) is a college admission test based on English, Math, Social Studies, Reading Skills and Scientific Reasoning.

AP (Advanced Placement Program) the College Board allows students to take college level courses while in high school. If the student scores high enough on the national exam, college credit may be granted for the course.

AWARD LETTER The document you receive from the college you have been accepted into and what that college is offering you financially.

CLEP (College Level Exam Program) allows testing for possible college credit for beginning college courses.

COLLEGE CREDIT passing the course counts towards a college degree.

COMMON APPLICATION a number of colleges use this application for admittance.

COST OF ATTENDANCE the total expenses before financial aid.

DEMONSTRATED NEED the difference between your EFC and cost of attendance.

DUAL ENROLLMENT while students are enrolled in high school they may take a college level class at the same time. Often taught by a high school teacher at their high school.

EFC OR EXPECTED FAMILY CONTRIBUTION the cost for college the family is expected to pay. It is computed by a national formula determined by filing the Free Application for Federal Student Aid.

ENROLLMENT STATUS based on the number of credit-hours you have taken.

EXTRA-CURRICULAR ACTIVITIES students do outside of normal classroom courses.

FAFSA (Free Application for Federal Student Financial Aid) the form that must be completed by the family that determines the family's expected contribution.

FINANCIAL AID the money given to students to help pay for college, such as Grants, loans and scholarships.

529 SAVINGS PLAN a state-sponsored investment plan to help families save money for college (we do not recommend this plan)

GRANT financial aid that does not have to be paid back.

HONORS PROGRAM an opportunity for students to take challenging high school classes.

IB (International Baccalaureate Program) only available at high schools who have qualified to offer this program. It allows college level subject area curriculum based on global interpretation.

LOAN money you borrow that must be paid back with interest.

MERIT AID financial aid given to students based on their personal achievements.

NAIA (National Association of Intercollegiate Athletes) an association that governs communication between college coaches and student players at small schools.

NCAA (National Collegiate Athletic Association) an association that governs communication between college coaches and student players' at large schools.

NEED-BASED FINANCIAL AID financial aid given to students because they and their families are not able to pay the full cost of attending.

NEED-BLIND ADMISSION college admission decision without the knowledge of the applicants' financial situation.

NET PRICE the true amount a student will pay for a college.

NET PRICE CALCULATOR an online tool that gives you a personalized estimate of what it will cost to attend a specific college.

NSCAA (National Small College Athletic Association) an association that governs communication between college coaches and student players at very small schools.

OUTSIDE SCHOLARSHIP a private scholarship offered by a private organization, not the government or college.

PRIORITY DATE the date by which your application must be received to be given the best consideration.

RESERVE OFFICERS' TRAINING CORPS (ROTC) offered by the military and available at some colleges that offer scholarships to student who agree to serve in the military after they graduate.

RESIDENCY REQUIREMENTS the amount of time a student has to live in a state before he or she is eligible for in-state tuition.

STUDENT AID REPORT (SAR) the report sent to families after they submit the FAFSA that explains what the EFC is.

Made in the USA
Middletown, DE
31 January 2022

60102337R00096